ROME
PAST AND PRESENT

ROME
PAST AND PRESENT
TEXT BY
WILLIAM GAUNT

EDITED BY GEOFFREY HOLME

LONDON: THE STUDIO LTD., 44 LEICESTER SQUARE, W.C.2

1926

PRINTED AND ENGRAVED BY HERBERT
REIACH, LTD., EYOT WORKS, ST.
PETER'S SQUARE, HAMMERSMITH,
LONDON, W.6

CONTENTS

ILLUSTRATIONS

(* Denotes Illustrations in Colour)

LIST OF ARTISTS REPRESENTED

Erratum.—Plate XXXIII, a Sixteenth Century Engraving, is wrongly attributed to Alessandro Specchi.

EDITOR'S NOTE

Grateful acknowledgment is made in the first place to His Majesty the King, for graciously according permission to reproduce three drawings by Canaletto in the Royal Collection. The Editor also desires to express his thanks to the private collectors, artists, and museum authorities, British and foreign, who have assisted him in the preparation of this volume; he is especially indebted to the Duke of Devonshire, the Duke of Wellington, Lord Ellesmere, Lord Sandwich, Sir Herbert Cook, Sir Harry Wilson, Lady Witt, Col. D. S. Morton, Mrs. W. Gaunt, and Messrs. Arthur Kay, A. G. H. Macpherson, May, S. Morse, P. Turpin; to the authorities of the Royal Geographical Society and the Royal Institute of British Architects: and to Messrs. P. & D. Colnaghi & Co., J. Connell & Son, Ltd., Insel Verlag, and D. Croal Thomson.

The Editor has taken full advantage of the great collection of reference prints in the library of Sir Robert Witt, of whose aid he desires to make special acknowledgment.

 HE city of Rome is a kind of central dais in a great arena. Some such figure of speech is a necessary translation of geography. The Campagna is very like a titanic theatre whose walls are the Alban and the Sabine mountains, a theatre in which many a strange audience has assembled to watch the making of history and sometimes to mount upon the stage and take part therein. That sense of power and majesty which Rome gives in itself is already apparent to the traveller long before he has come to its outskirts. The miles of dull plain are featureless. A few ragged eucalyptus trees are to be seen. A pelting farm which has been a monastery, or a fortress, or a Goth-plundered villa, or all three, and whose peasant misery is grotesquely guarded by grandiose columns and gates. A lonely horseman, like a South American cowboy (so Garibaldi must have looked) spurs after a plunging herd of bulls, wielding a long pole in his hand. An aqueduct, far away, seems to crawl over the ground, its arches sending a ripple of movement along its length. At last all detailed impressions fade into one void of an overpowering monotony of drab, baked earth and long grass that the sun has deprived of colour. Yet the monotony seems a prelude or introduction not unworthy. It is an historical monotony. The atmosphere of the Campagna is charged with the great events of the past. Without any conscious marshalling of knowledge, without mental notes of " Here marched on Rome the Gauls, and here later their descendants at the bidding of the Napoleons : here Hannibal and swarthy Carthaginians circled doubtfully about their prey "—one feels it all. History is audible in the silence of the place and implicit in its sadness. This Campagna was once populous and healthy. It has been the camping ground of warlike and migratory nations. It has held a tumultuous life. Its present state is not the negation but merely another aspect of these things.

To the East is the line of the Sabine hills, and to the South the Alban hills, which define the horizon sufficiently to emphasise the extent of the plain. The river Tiber takes a winding course across it and through the Sabines, and on the series of gentle eminences about twenty miles from its mouth is the city itself. Rome is not a city of a river ; it would be impossible, for instance, to compare the narrow and turbid Tiber with the Thames which, in a way, makes London what it is. It has no maritime advantage like Venice. In spite of its Seven Hills it has nothing resembling the hill of the Athenian acropolis. It is essentially

1

a city of the plain : and so for a general view one must ascend some of the neighbouring heights, and see it as Richard Wilson did in his view from Monte Mario.

So the Latin shepherds who were eventually to dominate the Ancient world looked down on the site of Rome from their rude settlements on the Alban slopes (the present Castel Gandolfo may be taken as their starting point). The gentle plateaux below were suited for pasture. The flocks wandered on in a north-westerly direction. The typical table-land became a centre of population. It was dedicated to Pales, the goddess of cud-chewing. Its sides were moderately steep, and so afforded protection against attack. The Palatine Hill in this way became the nucleus of the city. The legend of Romulus and Remus, and how these mythical foundlings and founders were suckled by a wolf is very pretty. But it is the romantic fabrication of a literary age : possessing not even a symbolic relation to fact. Romulus and Remus must be relegated to a place somewhere between Hengist and Horsa and Gog and Magog, as the fabulous twins of popular story.

The situation of the dwellers on the Palatine was defensible but not by any means impregnable. The Campagna was peopled by the Etruscans, a short, stout race of Asiatic character and gloomy temperament who undoubtedly resented immigrant shepherds : so that there is every likelihood that the city was fortified from the very beginning and that the life of its inhabitants was conditioned partly by war with the Etruscans and partly by admixture with them. Though Roman historians do not say so, for like all other peoples the Romans embellished and decorated their annals to their own greater glory, it is indeed likely that for a considerable period they suffered the indignity of Etruscan domination and that " war " then consisted of an attempt to shake off the yoke. Other shepherd communities, too, must have caused war, for example, neighbours so close as the Sabines, and the many early settlements on the other tablelands which intersect the Campagna. That the situation eventually crystallised out into an indisputable fact called Rome was due to a special advantage of position on a navigable river and the trading route to the sea : and to the old recipe of *vi et armis*. At all events the foundations must have been laid about a thousand years before Christ of that stubborn martial character which came to be the main feature of the Roman and impressed itself upon every kind of civic activity which he undertook, giving even to his tombs the appearance of strongholds and the possibility of being used for that purpose. The " gravitas " or phlegm, the heavy, serious quality of mind expressed in a heavy, serious architecture, may have been acquired from the Etruscans : the full faced heavy-jowled types which are to be seen in surviving portrait busts points to an admixture.

2

Etruscan influence also gave to Roman architecture one of its most prominent motives—the round arch. The Cloaca Maxima, whose orifice is still to be seen and over whose stones the sewage of a thousand years has passed, is characteristic of Etruscan masonry.

WALLS.—Thus growing amidst danger and battle, Rome had of necessity to possess a defensive wall, at first no doubt a wooden stockade which was elaborated in more enduring material. The scattered blocks of stone which take us back farther than any other actual remains into the city's past are the remains of walls, and the wall continues to be an index of development throughout ancient times. The earliest traces are as we should expect, on the first settled hill, the Palatine, blocks of tufa, a volcanic mixture of ash and sand, the natural material of which the hills are composed. Down to the later days of the Republic the priests of the Lupercalia used solemnly to go through the traditional rite " beating the bounds," as it were, of *Roma Quadrata*. *Roma Quadrata* gave way as a community to a union of seven hills, the *Septimontium* (the Capitol being excepted). The final fusion of the various communities is marked by the Servian Wall, one of whose fragments is to be seen close to the Railway Station. The wall attributed to Servius Tullius may be dated between the third and fourth century B.C. From the Porta Capena, one of its gateways, at the foot of the Coelius, ran the oldest and most famous of Roman roads, the Via Appia. By the first century B.C. the wall had become a nuisance, and was subjected to assault from within. The increasing population surged over it, and in the Augustan period its course could not even be traced. Empire meant security, and for a long period Rome remained a perfectly open city—as open as London. Italy was composed of loyal colonies. The battles were fought, like those of England, in distant countries. Then in the third century A.D., when the frontiers were beaten down and the barbarians swarming over the Lombard plains, it was necessary to start all over again with the building of another wall. The Servian symbolises the danger of the city in its youth, the Aurelian wall the danger of its age. This huge *enceinte* covered half as much ground again as its prototype. The city now extends only in a very few places beyond it, and in other parts does not cover the area within. With its towers, and loopholed, battlemented walls, it seems to provide already a foretaste of mediæval existence, though in the Middle Ages it was manned only by hermits who paid a modest rental for the privilege of leading a life of meditation in its niches. By its *Porta Salaria* the Goths entered Rome, and even in the nineteenth century it was still to serve as a defence in the terrific Garibaldian episode of 1848—literally a nine days' wonder. Of the old Porta Ostiensis (now the Porta di San Paolo) a modern Italian artist gives us an excellent idea (Plate CXLIV).

FORA.—The obvious ground for fraternisation of the people who lived on the various hills was that low-lying quarter which was to be famous as the Forum. By its situation it was eminently well adapted to be a social and commercial centre, and as a meeting ground it must have assumed at a very early date the special odour of sanctity which it always possessed for the Romans. It has now a very sad and neglected appearance. It was battered by the religious enthusiasts of the Middle Ages, used as a quarry for the builders of the Renaissance, and as a culminating slight—completely forgotten. Being covered by the slow accretions of time it was called, until the nineteenth century inaugurated a period of excavation, the Campo Vaccino or Field of Cows. Under this title we see it represented in a whole series of paintings and engravings, for example, in Claude's painting in the Louvre which we reproduce. It is interesting, too, to note in his drawing of the Arch of Constantine how earth is piled up round it (Plate XXIII). Down to the last century we see in such representations only the tops of columns and arches buried under some thirty feet of rubbish. At the best of reconstruction the aspect of the Forum is sufficiently dismal, *Perierunt etiam Ruinae*. Its great columns are broken and isolated stumps. Its great buildings are reduced merely to ground plans. It is perhaps more difficult here than anywhere else in Rome to reconstruct its past in the imagination. Yet here centred all religious, social, commercial interests and activities, and here the richest of the architectural arts were employed. Had this essay been written a century earlier it would have contained at this point some sound moralising on so striking an instance of the vanity of human wishes and the impermanence of human memorials. The Forum was to Rome in a way what Westminster is to London, or rather we must imagine a combination of the Houses of Parliament, Westminster Abbey, the Law Courts, the Caledonian Market, and a big football ground, to arrive at a comprehensive parallel. It included temples, basilicas, memorial sculpture, a stadium, and booths where all kinds of business were transacted. Robbers would dispose of their gains in the open, merchants would arrange their big deals in the basilicas, wild beast fights would amuse the crowd. Hard-faced politicians, looking very like *American* senators (an examination of a large number of surviving portrait busts will bear out the comparison) discussed their plans in the Forum, and here too came strolling the typical *flaneur* of softer mould like Horace, eager for a little light conversation and amusement. The Forum summed up the life of the city—a fact which helps to explain its mournful character now.

4

When we say " Forum " we refer, of course, to the Forum Romanum, a slow and natural accretion of buildings and tradition. There were other Fora, designed as complete decorative areas by the Emperors, and with the especial purpose of testifying to their own divine character and prodigality of public favours. Julius Cæsar constructed such a forum, but of this nothing now exists. Adjoining it was, and is, the Forum of Augustus. It was bounded by a great wall, which Piranesi has drawn in the Vedute. We reproduce a modern version of its appearance by Mr. Sydney Lee (Plate CXXIV) which shows clearly its deviation from the straight, a feature which may have been due to the fact that private owners did not wish to give up their property or that it would have cost too great a sum to buy them out. The height and thickness of the wall are also to be noted. It is a curious thing that Ancient Rome even in its most marmoreal phase suffered from frequent and terrible fires, and the wall was so constructed as a barrier against them. At the north end of the Forum stood the Temple of Mars Ultor, flanked by a colonnade. The walls on each side curved outwards, in a kind of bastion. The Forum was in its origin a great memorial to the battle of Philippi. Otherwise it served for the hearing of legal cases crowded out of the main court. Then there is the Forum of Nerva, built by Domitian between that of Augustus and the Forum Pacis, which contained a Temple of Janus and had an outer wall fronted by columns, which are still to be seen half buried (Piranesi, Plate LXXXII, Prout, Plate CV). Lastly came the Forum of Trajan, the biggest of all, which commemorates the Emperor's victory over the Dacians. To make it, the stupendous work was undertaken of removing the high ground connecting Capitol and Quirinal. A vast square with colonnades, a vast Basilica, the Basilica Ulpia, a great record office of works in Greek and Latin, infinite statuary, and the column devoted to the Emperor were among its wonders, which dazzled and delighted contemporaries. Hadrian added the filial offering of a temple. For an idea of what remains we may turn to Sir Charles Eastlake's picture (Plate XCVI).

TEMPLES.—The general type of Roman temple, that which we find in very splendid shape in the fora, has nothing peculiar in principle to Rome. It is like the Greek temple with the addition of ornate detail, rectangular in shape, and possessing a similar arrangement of columns, save that the portico is generally deeper. We find that the columns are at once slenderer and less graceful, and that the Corinthian capital though often delightful has not the subtlety of the Greek Doric or Ionic. The Greek temple seemed to grow naturally out of its site, to be a part of the mountains, and intended to provide enchanting glimpses of the wine-dark sea in the interstices of its outline. The Greeks worked with

5

a landscape before them that in itself demanded a chaste and delicate simplicity of silhouette. The Romans became enamoured of the form without paying much attention to the circumstances of its setting (like English architects in the first phase of the nineteenth century). They spoiled in their rectangular temples the Greek rigour of æsthetic form, grafting on much impertinent detail, and increasing the size with a confused purpose of imparting grandeur. The grandeur we can see to more advantage in their other types of building : and the subtler qualities are lost. The present remains of the rectangular temples are, however, very fragmentary, and there is nothing (save perhaps the temple of Fortuna Virilis) at Rome to match the Maison Carrée of Nîmes, which shows an exceptional refinement. There is a portion of the front of the Temple of Saturn in the Forum, three fine columns of the Temple of Vespasian, richly fluted, three fine columns of the Temple of Castor and Pollux (Plate LXI). Here the senate often met, and the most important affairs were discussed. The wretched Caligula, it is said, was wont to place himself in between the statues of the Dioscuri in the hope that he also might be taken for a god. Three great columns remain of the Temple of Mars the Avenger, which was the depository of the crowns of the Roman conquerors and of the trophies they took in battle. The façade of the Temple of Antoninus and Faustina remains, now converted into the Church of San Lorenzo in Miranda, and surmounted by an ecclesiastical addition (Canaletto, Plate LVII, Cundall, Plate CXXXIX). The north side of the Temple of Neptune (founded after the Battle of Actium) is still an impressive sight as built into a former Custom House (Piranesi, Plate LXXIX). A study of the numerous other rectangular temples of which only the name or the plan now survive could serve no useful purpose here. We turn thence to two temples of quite a different kind which both in beauty and character far outweigh all the rest—the Pantheon and the little Round Temple on the Tiber.

In these two temples the Romans seem to be most themselves. There is no need to inquire too closely into the origin of the curving and spherical forms which are so well exemplified in them. The dead weight of a single dome entered naturally into their massive code of architecture. It may be a repetitive expression of the outer wall, a survival of the form of ancient burial tumuli, or part of the influence of the Hellenised East. It suffices to say that these two temples show a natural appreciation of what bold and magnificent curvature can effect : that the curve is repeated in most of the antique works that command our greatest admiration : and that it is a connecting link throughout the architectural history of the city, reappearing with an increasing fervour and licence finally in the Renaissance and the Baroque of the Eighteenth Century. In fact it is so essentially a classical and a Renaissance characteristic that

6

the modern revolt in art against the Renaissance has consisted in an antagonism to the curve—as in Cubism which conceives everything in terms of straight lines and angles.

The Pantheon, first erected in the reign of Augustus as a temple to Venus and Mars and afterwards reconstructed by Hadrian, that master-builder, is the masterpiece of religious art (we use the term advisedly) of Ancient Rome. Its present form is almost certainly due to Hadrian. It is a fortunate thing that so noble a building has come down to us in structural perfection. The bronze tubes formerly supporting the roof were removed by the Barberini Pope Urban for the Altar Canopy in St. Peter's, but their absence is not noticeable. Externally it has the mixed character usual to the race that is eclectic in matters of art (Plates LI and LX). The porch has no very close relation to the rotunda, the entablature stopping short. Its high gable and big pediment are in curious contrast to the flattened, Byzantine dome, though (to the present writer) this is rather pleasant than otherwise. The sixteen great Corinthian columns of the porch have a comforting amplitude at close quarters (Piranesi, Plate LXXXIII). Yet from the strictly æsthetic point of view the porch might have been dispensed with altogether. But in a very Byzantine manner the brilliance of effect is concentrated in the interior. Once the ancient doors of bronze are passed—as Stendhal said in his *Promenades dans Rome*, " on fait quelques pas, on voit l'église et tout est fini." The dome, cunningly panelled in a receding perspective soars upwards to the saucer of light which is the sky, and a single shaft of light completes the artistic unity of the composition. Dead weight though it is on walls made thick to withstand it, the dome communicates an impression of the utmost ease and lightness, and was likened by the Romans themselves to the vault of heaven. Niches in the interior contained great statues of the gods. All ancient colour and sculpture has, of course, long since disappeared. One does not regret it. It is true that the gods have been replaced by the tombs of the Renaissance (including the Tomb of Raphael) ; and by those of Victor Emmanuel II and the assassinated Humbert I (" tasteless tombs " as Baedeker might say) ; and by the decoration which signals the conversion of the place into " Santa Maria Rotunda." All this is powerless to distract the spectator, the whole effect is so final and absolute. Stendhal spoke the literal truth. Details are of no account. One takes three steps, beholds the dome, and lo ! there at least is one impression that will never fade. Pannini was inspired to one of his brilliant *tours de force* in depicting it (Plate LXIX). It is something of an anticlimax to come after this to the delightful little Round Temple on the Tiber, but this also goes to show how singularly happy the Romans were in dealing with the rotund form.

7

This temple, discounting the somewhat incongruous picturesqueness of modern roof, is quite exquisite. It is interesting to compare it with Bramante's *tempietto* in the cortile of San Pietro in Montorio.

BASILICAS.—The dome is traced to the Hellenised East. From the same quarter came the special form of building called *basilicas* which had their original model in the " Stoa Basilike " or Hall of Kings at Athens. The basilica was introduced at Rome in the second century A.D., and corresponded pretty closely to the modern Exchange, combining with this the function of court of law. It consisted of a great central hall flanked by side aisles divided by rows of columns and lit by high clerestory windows. It is necessary to imagine also a polychromatic effect of coloured marbles and decoration on the walls and pavement. There was in most cases a kind of annex, round in form, in which sat the court. The many basilicas vied with one another in splendour. The Basilica Julia in the Forum Romanum, the Basilica Ulpia in the Trajan Forum, the Basilica of Constantine, of which three great arches remain, like a great mountain, said Montaigne, split up into fearsome boulders (Schwabe, Plate CXXXI). There are now few other traces of these temples of commerce.

TOMBS.—A people of forceful and practical character, with a strong belief in property and the permanence of institutions, is usually lavish of memorial sculpture and architecture. The sceptical and modest Greeks were sparing of such things, and their references to death both in literature and art are of a very reticent kind. They preferred the gentle tribute of a sigh rather than ponderous masonry which did not appeal to their delicate humour. Nor were they bound in any way to the personal element in sculpture like the Romans who developed portraiture above everything else. The Roman, hating to think of the transience of life, demanded some lasting projection of the *ego*. The result was that many of the most striking landmarks of the ancient city were memorials to the individual. The Moles Hadriani is a prime example. This tremendous tomb has been greatly altered with the passage of time. The ancient cylinder was originally girdled with columns. Where the mediæval parapet now rests was a row of statues. In place of the mediæval and modern superstructure was a smaller cylinder. A statue of Hadrian in all probability occupied the present position of the Archangel Michael. Every ancient ornament has disappeared, and yet the body of the building survives in its original shape, but with all the aspect of a powerful fortress. The resting place of the Emperors became the last hope of their beleagured capital. What was built in sheer vanity came to have the grimmest of practical

8

uses : and it is curious to think of fierce and barbarous warriors swarming round this mausoleum turned blockhouse. Its warlike history takes us down from the time of the Goths to the time of Charles V who besieged the Castle in 1572, on which occasion Benvenuto Cellini claimed to have shot the Constable de Bourbon from the ramparts.

It was forbidden to build tombs within the city, and the rests of the Roman nobility lay in long rows of sepulchral architecture on the outskirts. The Via Appia, the Southern highroad paved with huge lava blocks, was lined for miles with tombs. One trundles now along its course in a battered *vettura*, and again the sad spell of the Campagna holds one at the sight of amorphous mounds that once gleamed with memorial marble but are now crusted with the crazy homes of labourers. The Tomb of Cæcilia Metella (Claude, Plate XIX) is solid enough to deceive the imagination for a moment, a fleeting point of time in which your cab becomes a smart chariot such as that in which the young Roman delighted to stir the Olympic dust. But such sprightly fancies do not long withstand the melancholy of it.

It was with the Romans, too, that the column and the arch became not only the supports of a building, but decorative features in themselves. The Romans liked, as well as the perpetuation of themselves, forms of art without any immediate usefulness—a trait of which in its later manifestations an excellent defence may and has been put up. On the Trajan Column it is merely vicious, however, the long winding relief being carved with painstaking detail in a position where it is impossible for people to see it (Plate VI). The Trajan Column, the Column of Marcus Aurelius (Plate V), and the Column of Phocas are the chief examples. With (in the case of the first two) remote (and now usurping) stylites, they have little save historical interest.

The Imperial apotheosis is awkwardly represented at best by placing a statue on the top of a very tall column. But the arch so massive and strong with its sense of unyielding power is undoubtedly impressive. Of this embodiment of the favoured semi-circular motive there exist many fine examples which have been painted, drawn and etched by most of the artists who have visited the city (Plates XXI, XXIII). The Arch of Constantine, the tribute to a Christian Emperor is perhaps the best of them, though it has some curious discrepancies of decoration. This, the Arch of Titus (Plate CXIII), the Arch of Severus (Plate LIX), and the Arch of Janus defy the onslaughts of time. Their sculptured panels are amongst the most important of documents. They are not in the accepted sense beautiful, but prime specimens of the ruler art, heavy handed and dominant.

THEATRES.—We have spoken of the Pantheon as the most artistic

9

building of Ancient Rome. The Colosseum is the most tremendous and in a sense the most typical. As the English take their pleasures sadly, so the Romans took theirs in grim earnest, building a place of amusement that would last for ever. The truly remarkable nature of the fact can only be realised by a comparison. Imagine, shall we say, a West End cinema that would in the year 3776 be the astonishment of the world; that would, subsequently to the fall of the British Empire, so completely lose its purpose as to be regarded as a temple; that would be used as a fortress, and then ruthlessly pillaged for building materials to make houses and palaces galore; that would at the end of this destructive process still appear intact and awe inspiring. In this way one would have an exact analogy with the history of the Flavian amphitheatre. This building which stands for at least one half of our notion of the classical world is immensely picturesque, and appealed especially for that reason to Byron and Goethe and their picturesque-loving generation. It is very rarely that we hear its proportions praised or, indeed, think of it at all as possessing intrinsic æsthetic qualities. It satisfied in its creators a craving for the stupendous and their ambitions were probably like those of the American maker of skyscrapers, though they expanded horizontally rather than vertically. The Virgilian sneer and exhortation was deeply rooted in the Roman humility. Leave to others the subtleties of art. *Tu regere imperio*—stone as well as peoples. If they could not help being imperfect they would at any rate be marvellously so. The imperfection for that matter explains the great practical influence of Roman architecture as compared with that of the Greeks. The latter is too final to be imitated. But the Romans were excellent models because imperfect: they could be improved upon, altered and adapted.

The Colosseum (Plates LXXXV, CXI) is picturesque from many points of view. The crumbling and piercing of its great blocks of travertine —think of slaves groaning and bullock carts straining with these burdens —has produced that effect of varied decay which Prout and the English water-colourists loved to depict. It is a romantic thing to stand in the arena and people the broken tiers with a roaring mob; to picture some bloated emperor lolling in the *Pulvinar*, a great awning creaking over-head and golden with the sun, desperate men at work with the *gladium* and beasts snarling in the ominous recesses. It is supremely picturesque by moonlight—*im mondschein*, one almost hears Geothe ecstatically crooning. It is possible almost to persuade the ghost of Nero into appearance, and an eerie throng in the places where seats should be. The vein of reflection is somewhat trite—often thought and much better expressed elsewhere. But the author must place on record one personal impression—that of a company of pilgrims singing some devotional

10

chant that was like the pæan of triumph sung by martyrs that awaited their doom. One momentarily expected a Nubian lion to spring into their midst. The walls frowned down uncomprehending, and the whole scene was vastly sweet and emotional—a sudden focussing of the pervading contrast between the Pagan and the Catholic city.

Of the other great theatres and circuses of Rome there are comparatively few remains. There were many stadia in which games and public performances took place. The floating populace, one of the unfortunate results of a top-heavy civilisation, diligently attended. *Panem et circenses*—free bread and plenty of entertainment—the modern implication is a little too obvious to be dwelt upon. The Theatre of Marcellus almost rivalled the Colosseum. At its dedication alone 600 lions were slaughtered, and most expensive shows of all kinds were given there. It was occupied in the Middle Ages by the Pierleoni after whom it was then named. It was taken over in the fourteenth century by the Savelli who built it up as a dwelling house. Since their time it has been continuously occupied. Poor people live behind the imperial façade and in between the crumbling columns. To see a deserted Roman ruin is impressive, but to thread one's way through the narrow alleys of the Ghetto and behold a ruin inhabited, with tiny shops burrowed into the purulent cliff of masonry, touches the imagination with a peculiar appeal (Plate XCII).

The beast and gladiatorial shows took the place of the modern theatre. The baths took the place of the modern club. They were very numerous—Baths of Agrippa, Nero, Titus, Trajan, Caracalla, Decius, Diocletian, all large and splendidly equipped. They formed communal meeting places where men of leisure would foregather, in fact conforming in many respects to the standards of Pall Mall combined with the ritual of the modern Turkish bath. There was the hot room, or Calidarium, where one perspired, the Tepidarium, where one washed in lukewarm water, followed by the cold bath in the Frigidarium. These three divisions of the bath were the nucleus, and around them extended reading rooms, gymnasia and stadia. One can picture what glorious smoking rooms would have been adjoined if the Romans had but known of the blessed weed. The ruins of the Baths of Caracalla are the most extensive and impressive, and most artists have felt the fascination of this pile of masonry. From its present state we deduce great columnate walls covered with marble of many colours; pavements richly set with mosaics; lunettes high above admitting light. The baths covered an enormous area, a fact which testifies to their civic importance. A few fragments of mosaic and marble still cling to the structure. The pipes of the hypocaust can still be seen. Nothing new under the sun—not even central heating. With the Romans cleanliness may be said to have been next to ungodliness, and the luxury of their bathing has been suggested as a contributing cause of their downfall. A feeling of luxury still hovers over the Baths of Caracalla even in their barren and unroofed condition (Plate CXXXIII).

PRIVATE HOUSES AND PALACES.—Primitive Rome was an aggregation of shepherd huts of the type which is shown in later burial urns—possessing a conical thatched roof and wide door supported by rough columns. In its next phase it had the aspect of an Italian provincial town, whose Puritanical inhabitants lived in meagre houses bare of ornament and huddled together behind their protective wall as in mediæval Nüremberg. This condition persisted without substantial alteration until the time of the wars with Carthage, which in the outcome gave Rome the mastery of the sea and a consequent expansion of Mediterranean trade. The population began to increase then and to spread beyond the Servian wall with suburban houses and gardens on the outskirts. Empire grew, and the luxury products of the East and of the North of Africa poured into the capital, so that Augustus is said to have found the city of brick and left it of marble. A general air of luxury began to prevail in the first century A.D. With luxury came the usual difficulties. At the height of the Imperial period the population had grown to about a million—an eighth of the present population of Greater London, but enough to create acute problems. The people flocked in from the neighbouring country when it ceased to be profitable to raise cereals, and had, in spite of enormous ground rents, somehow to be housed. The problem was left to take a muddled and unguided course, as it was in Victorian London, and tall blocks of jerry-built flats or *insulae* came into being. How perishable these poor dwellings were is shown by the very frequent records of fires; and most of them deserved to perish. The fire of 64 A.D., during which Nero "fiddled," was very probably as salutary as the Great Fire of London, destroying many abominable districts and enabling Nero to plan fresh quarters on improved lines—a fact for which he must be allowed some credit. It is impossible, of course, for us to give (except by an imaginary reconstruction) any actual illustration of the houses of the poor or the aspects of the city apart from its public buildings; but it is likely that they had a local character which would not remove them very far in general appearance from the Roman tenement house of to-day.

From the "free" people's homes we take a big jump to the houses of the nobility. There was in the Imperial age a proportion of one palace to about twenty-five ordinary dwelling houses. Of the upper class dwellings little survives in good condition. There is the House of Livia (so-called) on the Palatine—but for a detailed consideration of

12

well-preserved houses the traveller must go to Pompeii. In these we see well exemplified the florid Roman taste for polychromy and elaboration of ornament which provides a link with the taste of the Renaissance. It is somewhat vulgar, when all is said and done, though Pompeii was particularly inclined, we must suppose, to vulgarity, having always that flavour of " nouvelle richesse " which made it a kind of classical Palm Beach. The better sort of Roman preferred a villa in the hills amidst peaceful and picturesque surroundings—another link with the Renaissance.

The Palatine was the home of the " palace," whence indeed comes the name. Here Augustus built one great residence and Tiberius another. The latter building remains. One can still see the ruins of the passage in which Caligula was murdered. Nero built for himself a Golden House on the Esquiline—a marvellous pleasure dome with endless lakes and gardens. Here under a mysteriously rotating cupola made to resemble the solar system we picture this amazing dilettante singing execrably, playing indifferently on musical instruments, and taking vice and the arts as seriously as only an ancient Roman could.

A brief impression of the aspect of ancient Rome must end with a reference to its really first-rate civic administration. The roads that led into the city were models. Some of the ancient bridges, the Pons Ælius (the Ponte San Angelo, Plate XCIV) and the Pons Fabricius (Plate CXXIX), for example, still stand without substantial alteration. The water supply was admirable—it is a special feature which persists to this day—and the great aqueducts which carried water from the hills testify to an admirable organisation even though they were strategically unsound. Artists give us only ruins. Literature and scientific reconstruction recall the dazzling luxury of cool marble colonnades, innumerable plashing fountains, superbly ornate temples and theatres. We must touch in the picture with the impression of noisome alleys in which lived a filthy Mediterranean rabble out of all touch with the standards of Cato the Censor. After all, perhaps the ruins have the best of it. The slum element has disappeared, and so too has the ornamentation of the greater buildings. What remains is the simple fabric, which is like its makers, stripped as they might be stripped of a thin veneer of alien culture : possessing Republican dignity and austerity : sheer strength and power. The ruins tell us the truth.

MEDIÆVAL ROME.—The overlapping of Imperial and Christian Rome is one of the outstanding paradoxes of history. It is hard to realise the synchronism of the decadent pagan city and the sect which was to outlast force by its stubborn mildness : and it seems expedient to carry on the account of the external beginnings of Christianity to our

13

sketch of the mediæval city. The first visible and outward sign of Christianity in terms of bricks and mortar is the system of Catacombs— the subterranean burial places whose amazing galleries stretch one above the other for mile after mile under the Campagna. It is not accurate, however, to consider them entirely as a desperate refuge from persecution. Christianity was first regarded by the Roman official as a mild eccentricity, a provincial foible which could be connived at so long as it did not assume any political influence. But, as it developed, its democratic tendency caused it to be regarded as a dangerous enthusiasm. The Catacombs had their origin in the general law of the city which decreed that all tombs should be placed outside its limits. Services were held there openly at first. Then the place was hallowed by persecution : and after the persecution had stopped, the Catacombs had become an official and sanctified institution, and were vastly extended for that reason alone and no other.

Having been long forgotten, the Catacombs were rediscovered in the sixteenth century, and their leagues of galleries explored. Into the dim recesses the casual visitor now penetrates for a few yards by the light of a flickering taper. Tiny cavities indicate the place of tombs over which some πρεσβεία περὶ χριστιανῶν once murmured a primitive service in the underground gloom. The Christian symbols are painted and incised on the wall, and the image of Christ looks down—the traditional and unmistakable likeness which in some mysterious manner has impressed itself universally and beyond power of change upon the whole of European art. One approaches a party of peasants to whom a priest gives his stereotyped recital—their awestruck bearded faces, uncouth gestures, lit darkly by candles, make a picture not to be forgotten—a painting by Caravaggio. Strangely enough, though the Catacombs have such a chequered history ; though they have seen the epilogue of many an event of horror ; though Goths have been here roughly searching for the bones (and ornaments) of saints ; though they are dark and carved out far beneath the surface of the earth ; their effect is not in the least uncanny. One seems on the other hand to perceive a pervading atmosphere of calm and content. Perhaps after all something of human character passes into the walls of the places men build and frequent, and the Catacombs hold in suspense an impalpable essence of the Christian spirit. In the open air again one may look down a long grove of trees to where the dome of St. Peter's shines in the sun. It is another of Rome's contrasts—this turning from the virginal commencement of faith to its ultimate efflorescence.

How Rome fell, and even if it may be said to have really fallen at all, is one of those questions on which the historian loves to argue and often to be perverse. The modern historian will thus sometimes maintain

14

that it did not fall : which is only true if by that he means that there was no apocalyptic destruction such as John Martin might have pictured ; no wrathful lightning and fires and sudden consuming by a lurid combination of divine and barbarian wrath. If he means that the process was gradual, it is possible to agree with him. As long as Rome stood for the whole of the civilised world there was not much point in revolting against it ; it was merely a question of who should rule it. The trouble was that this important point in itself entailed war and destruction, whatever reverence may have filled the breasts of contending parties. The Goths may have admired Rome, but they had to fight in order to win it. In this manner destruction became the sincerest form of flattery. Theodoric the Goth, for instance, ruled Italy with efficiency and success, and did not wish to disturb the system which had previously worked so well. Under his direction agriculture improved, and a semblance of prosperity was recovered. To offset this, we have the fact that Rome suffered terribly while Theodoric was getting command—that the aqueducts were cut in order to stop the city's water supply ; that the outlying villas became ruined and deserted ; that the Campagna was turned into the malarial marsh which it is even now. The Campagna had, it is true, a long record of fever, and there were ancient altars to Mefitis or Verminum, " the god of microbes," to use Lanciani's phrase. But the Imperial age had seen it largely cleansed by irrigation works. This was to go for nothing.

In fact, the aspect of the city was radically changed, and its magnificence blotted out. The removal of the capital to Byzantium deprived it of material importance. Later in the Middle Ages the removal of the Popes to Avignon deprived it of spiritual importance. As time went on the city sunk lower and lower in the scale. The works of antique art were thrown into the melting pot. There was a rapid disappearance of all perishable structures. Moveable spoils were distributed among a population of thieves and cut-throats. Jan Both's " Popular Life at Rome " (Plate XXV), though, of course, a seventeenth-century work, well expresses this sinister atmosphere. The greater of the ancient buildings were constantly pillaged for materials, just as a forest might provide the material for log cabins. Good examples of the pitiful result are those which Sr. Carbonati has etched for us (Plates CXIV, CXVII). The mediæval " casette " is a humble assemblage of unconsidered trifles, and the Casa dei Rienzi a grotesque and absurd collection of splendid odds and ends which has the appearance more of a Maya temple than anything else. What was imperishable was utilised as a fortress. The tomb of Hadrian became the Castle of San Angelo. A miraculous apparition as of the Archangel Michael sheathing his sword above the tower, which was seen in 590, gave it its abiding name. We

15

illustrate the episode from the Sforza Book of Hours in the British Museum (Plate II). Though the place was taken over by the Pope, whose sumptuous apartments form the superstructure, it long retained the character of stronghold and prison. There are some grim little chambers in one of which once lay Beatrice Cenci, Shelley's dark heroine, and Benvenuto Cellini, that self-made hero, to whom it gave as great an autobiographical opportunity as the Venetian Prison under the Leads to Casanova. For a surprising picture of the Castle, with a mad keeper, we refer the reader to Cellini's Memoirs. The building has always attracted the topographical artist. One of Falda's large plates, here reproduced, gives a fine view looking along the bridge (crowded by Bernini's statues) with a luxurious papal procession. A side view (Plate XXXIII) (a century earlier) shows both the castle and the bridge without its present statues (the angel was not installed until the eighteenth century), and Piranesi's view (Plate LXXIV) from the rear shows the secret passage constructed by the Popes and the collection of military equipment attached to the building. Vernet (Plate LXXX) paints the Castle looking down the river, enlivening the sullen Tiber with a gay water tournament in the Venetian manner. Richard Wilson draws (Plate XCIV) the most celebrated view of all, looking upstream, in which the dome of St. Peter's combines with the great drum of the castle in a most pleasing composition.

As well as the Castle, the Colosseum became in the Middle Ages a stronghold of the Roman barons, and down to the eighteenth century the haunt of ruffians who made it dangerous of approach. It was infested by an almost infra-human race, wild figures such as Piranesi sometimes drew. As we have mentioned, the Theatre of Marcellus became a fortified dwelling house, and the Arch of Titus became a bastion of the Frangipani. In the sixteenth century Flemish drawing in the Witt Collection, the Arch of Severus shows a curious loft built on the top—a transitory feature—compare Piranesi's plate of the same subject. Other ancient buildings were turned into churches. The tradition of sanctity was especially kept up in the various temples of the Forum, by a sort of revenge, the Temple of Romulus, for instance, becoming in the sixth century SS. Cosma e Damiano. At that period there was still a kind of religious triumph held in the Forum in the pontifical processions. The Temple of Antoninus and Faustina became S. Lorenzo in Miranda in the seventh century (Canaletto, Plate LVII). The Macellum Magnum built by Nero became in the fifth century S. Stefano Rotondo. The Round Temple on the Tiber was converted into S. Maria del Sole in the twelfth century. The Pantheon became used for religious purposes in the seventh century, and acquired the title of Santa Maria Rotunda.

16

This process of adaptation (and obscuration) was the most characteristic feature of mediæval Rome. There was no creative impulse whatsoever in the city. Other cities of Italy had a vigorous life in the Middle Ages. Rome merely existed. Whatever was actually done bore the classical stamp. The city had ceased to be a capital of anything save brigandage, and there was no inducement for artists to go there. The long barren period helps to explain why Rome even in the most prolific days of the Renaissance produced singularly few painters, sculptors or architects. The north of Italy had the advantage of a working tradition beginning with Cimabue and Giotto, and ending (in Florence alone) with Michael Angelo and Leonardo da Vinci. In any case, however, even Ancient Rome had little native talent, and what made it then and in the Renaissance period so magnificent in appearance was the work of artists attracted by the magnetic influence of wealth and appreciation. Art is not produced by riches, but is almost invariably to be found where riches are.

Well, the Christian basilica (in view of the principle from which we have wandered somewhat) has no original features, but is simply a special type of the pagan basilica—examples being S. Maria Maggiore (fifth century here), and S. Paolo fuori le Mura. The tradition was too strong and sensibility too sluggish even for such a subdued and saracenic Gothic style as we find at Venice. Vertical aspirations have never had a great appeal for the Italian. The Romanesque even, which both in name and character is very clearly related to the classical Roman architecture, is a rare thing on Roman ground. We find, of course, the typical details of the Romanesque—the campanile, the apse and the round porch. Claude has drawn for us the fine apse of SS. Giovanni e Paolo (Plate XVIII). The campanile of S. Maria in Cosmedin, S. Francesca Romana al Foro, and S. Maria Maggiore, of the twelfth, thirteenth and fourteenth century respectively, are fairly good examples, though not outstanding. The bird's-eye view of the seven principal churches of Rome by Antonio Lafrery (Plate IV), though it belongs to the sixteenth century, gives an interesting idea of Romanesque details (it is interesting to note in it, too, the unfinished St. Peter's). But of the distinctive design in which the originality of the Romanesque lies—that is, the bold three-dimensional character which we see in the Cathedral of Anagni and the Towers of San Gimignano, and relates the Romanesque to very recent modern experiments—Rome shows us little.

RENAISSANCE ROME.—The gradual return of Rome to its traditional pre-eminence after the singular dark period of the Middle Ages is marked by an increasing activity in building and, generally

speaking, in artistic life. We include in the term " Renaissance Rome "
both the early rebirth of classical art and its later development familiar
under the title of Baroque. There is, in any case, no real break between
the two phases—they merge slowly one into the other. The later phase
is, however, most clearly bound to Rome itself, and has left the most
decisive mark on its appearance. There was every reason that the city
should become the centre of this new artistic age. A complex of movements tended to produce in the artist a desire to study and adopt the
work of the ancients. The Renaissance may thus be described in an
artistic sense as a patriotic movement, repelling on the one hand the
barbarous Gothic style coming from the North and the Eastern influences
of Constantinople. With this inspiration artists turned to the ancient
capital, taking their motives from such remains as the decoration and
paintings of the Neronic Golden House and the arch erected to Septimus
Severus which stands against the church of S. Giorgio in Velabro.
(Many of the drawings of Renaissance architects have a special value
as a record of the ruins of Ancient Rome.) Then also Rome was
rehabilitated as the centre of religion. As soon as the Babylonish
captivity was over it assumed its old spiritual importance. The Popes,
as time went on, and, curiously enough as the attacks from without
became greater, became increasingly zealous in their desire to make
Rome the supreme spiritual power. They desired to employ every
material resource to this end. They were sufficiently wealthy to under-
take great schemes of improvement, and for the most part sufficiently
enlightened to employ the men most qualified to carry them out. The
artists loved antiquity, and the Popes desired that art should glorify the
Catholic faith. The combination of these two impulses produced a
fever of enterprise in the city, which as it went on continually gained
momentum. In the early Renaissance other cities of Italy showed as
much originality (and wealth of achievement) as Rome, if not more.
In the final stages of the movement Rome had become indisputably the
most important, and its new aspect a fresh model for Europe to copy.
The Vatican marks the end of the " captivity " at Avignon. Here in
1397 Gregory X established the Papal Palace, which was completed
about the middle of the following century by Nicholas V. We give some
aspects of the exterior (Plates XXX and XCVIII) which is somewhat non-
committal and devoid of character, and has very much the look of the
purpose for which Nicholas designed it, a central bureau or great block
of religious offices. Within, endless corridors and saloons contribute to
fill the spectator with the same kind of dreary amazement that the Louvre
imposes. Its interest, needless to say, centres in the works of Michael
Angelo and Raphael. The Sistine Chapel paintings are a marvellous
thing to come upon in the midst of much meaningless and sugary decora-

18

tion—the work of a demigod. The thunderous swirl of figures in the
" Last Judgment," and the lyric beauty of the smaller episodes of the
ceiling are, however, no matters to dilate on here. Nobody has
described them better than Vasari who relates also inimitably the whole
strange story. How the jealousy of Bramante and others forced the
commission upon the artist so that he might fail, being unskilled in
painting ; how marvellous was the stern and solitary persistence of the
artist ; how impatient the Pope who " was always asking him impor-
tunately when he would finish it." We picture this Pope very active
about the work of genius " mounting certain ladders with the assistance
of Michael Angelo," and a final procession to the Chapel to sing Mass
" to the great satisfaction of the whole city," and we must suppose the
equal dissatisfaction of Bramante and others. Raphael also contributes
to the greatness of the Vatican. His frescoes and decorations without
achieving or indeed aiming at the force of Michael Angelo appeal to
the modern by the completeness of their artistic invention and their
cultured style, qualities here to be seen at their finest pitch.
Having established a headquarters, the Popes had now to build a great
church. St. Peter's is the central point of the religious revival, and,
architecturally speaking, a noble failure. In an architectural system
which depended upon the co-ordination of every part of a building
under the guidance of a single brain, St. Peter's is something of an
anomaly. Its erection was spread over too long a period of time. Too
many people had a share in the design. It was begun by Bramante,
crowned by Michael Angelo, and completed by Bernini, leaving out
of account the lesser men who at one time and another took over the
superintendence of the fabric. If it had been finished by Bramante
who " made an endless number of designs " for Julius II and " put
his hand to the work with the intention that it should surpass in beauty,
art, invention and design, as well as in grandeur, richness and adorn-
ment all the buildings that had been erected in that city," then it would
have been homogeneous and complete. Michael Angelo's dome is in
itself of singular beauty, but its effect is spoilt by Carlo Maderna's
façade, which is high and oppressive without possessing any artistic
merits of its own. It is interesting to compare Piranesi's etching with
Pannini's painting of the view looking towards the façade. Piranesi
has obviously felt the awkwardness of the concealment of the dome,
and seems deliberately to have raised it ; while Pannini has given us (for
once) a more truthful and less artistic version, showing how the dome
crouches behind the façade. Bernini's colonnade is in itself magnificent,
but is slightly unsatisfactory in its conjunction with the church. The
obelisk is an inherited piece of rather stupid eclecticism which
Mr. Geoffrey Scott in his *Architecture of Humanism* somewhat surpris-

19

ingly takes to prove his point of a communal religious enthusiasm in the building activities of Rome. His principle is sound, but he might have found a better illustration. The thing fundamentally resolves itself into a riot of Latin excitement over a successful engineering feat. There seems little in the removal of an Egyptian obelisk from one side of the church to another to cause a great outburst of religious feeling. We read of the " thirty-five windlasses to set in motion the monstrous machine which was to raise it with strong ropes ; each windlass worked by two horses and ten men " (Plate LVI). It was heaved up, let down on rollers, and in the Autumn moved " by three great efforts " on to the pedestal made to support it. On a purely human basis of estimation it is probable that the " indescribable exultation " of the people was caused by the great scaffolding and the immense complication of windlasses we see in our engraving. They enjoyed it as the crowd always does enjoy this sort of novelty. The Pope himself undoubtedly attached a mysterious significance to it, " boasting that he had wrested this monument from the Emperors Augustus and Tiberius, and consecrated it to the Holy Cross." But substantially, this particular episode means absolutely nothing in religious life. From the artistic point of view the obelisk in its present position is not displeasing nor is it especially appropriate to its position. The exterior of St. Peter's, in all, has many beautiful features, but lacks the complete unity necessary to a supreme work of art.

The interior represents the full ecstacy of the Baroque style, being calculated to inspire awe and reverence by a complete capture of the senses. In this it is immensely successful. Although the opposition of vertical and horizontal is so strict that one hardly realises the enormous scale, it has a wonderful breadth of effect, and the more people there are in the church the more obvious this becomes. Compare Plate LVIII showing the space under the dome on a day of Jubilee, 1700, in which the dense throng actually seems to become an artistic complement of the building itself. On every pillar there is an interlacing of blue, white, and gold, and overhead and around there flutters a host of saints and cherubim. Pannini's picture in the Louvre gives an admirable impression of the huge perspective and this unrestrained richness of many-coloured ornament. It is an actual fact that to the devout believer the splendour of the church comes as a sort of divine revelation, and the marble and stone seem to bear a supernatural impress. It is amazing to see the pilgrims crowd the interior during the Holy Year, to see the lifelong dream of some remote Central European peasant realised as he casts round wondering eyes with the air of one who already has a foretaste of heaven. Devout black clad figures, whose silhouette recalls the pious painting of some early Flemish master, kneel upon the

20

pavement and kiss the toe of St. Peter, as countless generations before them have done (Hubert Robert, Plate XCIII).   To see all this is to realise the extraordinary force of the Catholic religion, which unites the people of many nationalities at one indubitable centre.

One gains an impression, too, that nowadays there is a greater sincerity and devotion than ever before : certainly the present year shows an extraordinary contrast with the typical Renaissance Jubilee.   Signor L. Rodocanachi in a recent volume, " Une Cour Princière à Rome pendant La Renaissance," has compiled a detailed and most interesting account of the Jubilee of 1473.   This was marked first by an assemblage of royal personages.   Eleonora of Aragon, daughter of the King of Naples (who was about to marry Ercole d'Este) was the first to arrive, and by the orders of the Pope the Cardinal Pietro Riario received her. His palace was decorated for the occasion with gold and silver and silk and damask, and a feast of fifty dishes prepared which lasted for seven hours.   Storks, cranes, peacocks, boars, sturgeon, a stag, and a bear roasted whole comprised the fantastic menu.   Rich gifts were offered to the Princess, and on the day of Pentecost she attended service at St. Peter's together with the Queen of Bosnia.   Then followed all kinds of symbolic shows and performances.   Cardinal Riario organised races. This ingenious ecclesiastic was, however, overcome by a surfeit of splendour, and died in January, 1474, at the age of twenty-eight.   Then arrived the King of " Dacia " (Denmark).   Once more gifts were interchanged, the King offering to the Pope the septentrional tribute of herrings and cod.   He was followed by the Duke of Urbino for whom Cardinal Giuliano della Rovere gave up his palace.   At Christmas, 1474, Sustus IV opened the holy door of St. Peter's as a sign that the year of Jubilee had begun.   The number of pilgrims in this year was, however, very disappointing, for war raged throughout Europe, and the Romans and people in neighbouring towns who had laid in an extra quantity of supplies for the pilgrims found themselves heavily overstocked.   The Pope issued a request to rulers in every quarter that they should give special facilities and protection to pilgrims passing through their dominions and that duties might be lowered for their benefit.   In January, 1475, the King of Naples appeared at Rome with an escort of seventy knights.   His professional instincts were not overcome by the solemnity of the time, and he took occasion to remark to the Pope his surprise at the sight of so many alleys and balconies in the capital suitable for ambuscades ; suggesting some revision of architectural plan which would be at once æsthetic and anti-revolutionary—open spaces which would be healthier in every sense of the term.   Towards the end of the year the Tiber overflowed its banks, and pilgrims were obliged to go to certain churches by boat. A year of Jubilee nowadays is neither

21

so luxurious, so aristocratic, or so chequered by accident. It is simple (or comparatively so), well organised and animated by a spirit totally distinct from that of the " Humanistic Age."

The term " Humanism " as applied to the aspect of the city is one which needs definition. Its usual meaning is that of " polite *learning*," that is to say, an outlook and standards based on the classical models. It applies particularly well to the character of the Popes of the earlier Renaissance, and to the architecture of the earlier Renaissance. Bramante, for instance, is essentially a Humanist architect. His delightful little Tempietto in S. Pietro in Montorio is an exquisite piece of " polite learning," accomplished and refined, and bearing every evidence of careful study. Bramante, however, cannot be regarded as a great originative force. There is a restraint throughout his work that shows too great a caution in adherence to his model, and though his buildings are excellent as Humanism they are no essential part of the rebirth of Rome itself. The Baroque style represents firstly enthusiasm and religion—qualities entirely alien to " Humanism." It represents intuition rather than learning, making a daring improvisation of certain salient features of ancient building instead of a scholarly presentation of the details of ancient building. It is imaginative rather than precise, infusing paradoxically a romantic life into classical forms. The steps which architecture takes from Bramante, through Michael Angelo and so to Bernini, are exactly parallel with the steps taken by religion from Leo X, through Julius II, and so to Sixtus V. The Popes of the early Renaissance would reverence and restore ancient buildings as Pius IV restored the Baths of Diocletian. A Sixtus V would ruthlessly destroy them for the sake of his own plans as he destroyed the last valuable remnants (Plate XIII) of the Septizonium of Severus. This was the new force in the Papacy, called into being in a tremendous reaction against the Reformation, a force that could destroy because it was creative. The Baroque Popes were men of zeal, intelligence and power. They dreamed of a city that should rise like a phœnix out of the ashes of its humiliation, and they made the vision a material fact. But they were not educated men as their predecessors were. Such is the difference between Humanism and Baroque.

It is to be noted moreover that the Papacy was the only possessor of wealth in Rome. There was no commercial aristocracy as at Venice. The revenue gained from the patrimony of St. Peter and the contributions of the faithful in every part of Europe paid for the reconstruction. There were, therefore, three types of activity in the seventeenth century, churches, palaces for the great religious families, and civic improvements. The Piazza del Popolo and the Piazza di Spagna are examples of the papal zeal for the general appearance of the city. The fountains which are so frequent and pleasant a feature show another side of it. Sixtus V and Paul V both constructed aqueducts, the heavy *Acqua Paolo* (Piranesi, Plate LXXXI) commemorating the latter's success.

Of churches there is an immense number. A not altogether successful façade was added to S. Giovanni Laterani (Plate XXXVI), of which we give another and more interesting view in the painting by Poussin (Plate XXVIII). The Church of Santa Maria Maggiore (Sixtus V and Paul V) is particularly good, and with the column in the piazza, its campanile and bold façade makes a diversified but very distinguished composition (Plates IV, LXX). The Gésu built by Vignola is a fine example of the late sixteenth century. The seventeenth century saw a greater departure from tradition with, amongst others, Borromini. He designed the curious S. Carlo alle Quattro Fontane, and the beautiful S. Agnese in the Piazza Navona (Plate LXXIII) with its interesting points of resemblance to our own St. Paul's. Other of the outstanding seventeenth century churches of Rome were built by Carlo Rainaldi, examples being the twin churches of S. Maria di Montesanto and S. Maria dei Miracoli which give so distinguished a character to the Piazza del Popolo (Plate LIII), and the refined little church of S. Maria in Pace which recalls Bramante (Plate CXXXIV). The style kept its vitality until about the middle of the eighteenth century when it began to be merely pompous as in the façade of S. Croce in Gerusalemme by Gregorini (Piranesi, Plate LXXVI).

PALACES.—The Baroque palaces show the style in its most austere mood. The later development of the Renaissance is not so highly accentuated as it is in the churches: that is, the Baroque is not greatly distinct from the earlier Renaissance. The Palazzo Farnese (Plate XXXIV) designed by Michael Angelo and San Gallo, a most majestic work, is an architectural type whose characteristics remain fundamentally the same. There are, of course, exceptions, such as the Palazzo Zuccari (late sixteenth century), which reaches the utmost limit of the fantastic. In this building, doors and windows have become yawning mouths set in grotesque sculptured faces. This freakish fancy is, however, of comparatively early date, and cannot be taken as a bombastic effort of decadence. In general the Baroque architects sought deliberately to impart the effect of heavy majesty and solemnity proper to Ancient Rome, and aimed, as far as the façade was concerned, at imposing perspectives rather than a superfluity of ornament. Ornament was concentrated in great sculptured scrolls and heraldic emblems placed here and there over the windows and doors (Piranesi, Palazzo Odescalchi, Plate LXXV). In the interiors we find gigantic

23

staircases again conceived with the imaginative perspective so dear to the Baroque period. The staircase which leads up to the garden of the Palazzo Barberini (Plate XLIII) by Borromini is another outstanding example. There are also great saloons specially designed to form picture galleries (an anticipation of mortality?), as in the Colonna and Doria Pamphili Palaces; and every incidental form of magnificence. Huge mirrors and candelabra, walls hung with tapestry, ceilings richly decorated with gilt, and paintings even fill one with a subtle emotion of dread, so solid are they and so unreal.

The social phase and counterpart of the period of religious enthusiasm was short-lived, and the sort of people who could fittingly inhabit these great palaces has completely disappeared. An artificial order of society upheld by certain special circumstances gave them being, which, having gone, one feels the palaces should have vanished too and left not a rack behind. "There are no main streets of trade," says Montaigne . . . nothing, but ecclesiastical palaces and gardens.

The villas of the period are important principally for their gardens, in which the Baroque fancy disported itself to great advantage. The formal groves are delightfully depicted in the Renaissance engravings we reproduce (Plates III, X and XI). Velasquez has given us in a famous picture a somewhat eerie corner of the Villa Medici, and Decamps in a really beautiful work the sense of peace and repose which emanates from the gardens of the Villa Pamphilia. Fountains were another form of art particularly adapted to the Baroque, and of these there are many extraordinary specimens at Rome in which art imitates great natural boulders, and carves out shells, and mermen, tritons, naiads, dolphins, every imaginable curving and writhing symbol of the movement of water. The great Fontana di Trevi in which a figure of Neptune stands, and a wall of water descends into a great basin, is the most ambitious and one of the most successful (Plate CXXIII). They take an amazing variety of forms—sea horses spouting, as in the Fontana dei Cavalli Marini at the Villa Borghese, mermen upholding a shell in the Fontana di S. Maria in Cosmedin, a ship, as in Bernini's *Barca*, or the grandiose quintuple streams of the Acqua Paola.

Finally, the Baroque style was by its nature well calculated to adorn the theatre. The truly astonishing picture by Pannini of a concert at Rome which we illustrate (Plate LXIV) gives an excellent idea of its dramatic possibilities and its appropriateness to the gay, periwigged, ornate audience.

There is one main figure in the Baroque movement who sums it all up, the man who was "made for Rome"—Bernini. Bernini (1598-1690) served under eight Popes. He displayed the greatest daring in composition combined with the most vivid and naturalistic treatment of

24

detail. He was without question absolutely sincere, sincere throughout to his art, and in his later days deeply absorbed in religion. His Piazza of St. Peter's is a wonderful piece of town-planning, displaying both subtle refinements of perspective and a simplicity of scheme. He made the most rhythmical and harmonious use of the ancient feature of the curve, well to be seen in the little church of S. Andrae del Quirinale (Plate LV). The vista he created in the Scala Regia of the Vatican became a model. His *Ecstacy of St. Theresa* is the essence of the fervour of the Counter Reformation. Turn where you will in Rome, there is Bernini, in the magnificent palace of the Barberini, in the fountain of the Piazza Navona, in angel and cherubs so light and graceful that their rounded forms take on an ethereal quality equal to that which the mediæval sculptors of Chartres sought to gain by elongation.

With the Renaissance and the revival of interest in ancient buildings for their own sake, as models to follow and monuments to reverence, begins the era of topography. We have Alo Giovannoli's extremely bad engravings, with their scurrying crowds of mysterious ecclesiastics, and also in the sixteenth century the more careful and interesting work of Scamozzi, Etienne du Pérac, and Lafrery who gives partly reconstructions and partly the appearance of actual ruins. In the next century begins a whole series of topographical prints of Rome Ancient and (then) Modern, published by Rossi, amongst which those by Specchi are particularly good. We have drawn considerably on these, and for purely illustrative purposes they are undoubtedly first-rate. Claude is on an entirely different plane of the seventeenth century, and his drawings, supremely beautiful as they are, never represent any strong interest in the buildings of Rome as such. Even when he follows architecture so closely as he does in the Apse of SS. Giovanni e Paolo (Plate XVIII) he is still abstract and unimpassioned. He pursues a strictly æsthetic purpose so that it is admissible to include his Rome drawings amongst topographical work only provided we do not mix our appreciation of their representing the city with our appreciation of Claude's art. Then in the eighteenth century we come to the topographical exponent of the Baroque in Piranesi, giant amongst architectural draughtsmen. A Venetian by birth he found his spiritual home in the capital, representing it with exactitude, industry, and a high order of imagination. His colossal compositions, his wild and picturesque detail, make his etchings the graphic complement of Bernini's architecture. Pannini is not such a great artist : nor has he always the secondary attribute of truthfulness, descending often to the destestable practice of grouping several ruins together according to the dictates of a sentimental fancy. His pictures are full of detail, but not such good detail as that which Canaletto or even Guardi provides. Nevertheless, Pannini is excellent fun, and has to his

25

credit two quite amazing interiors of the Pantheon and St. Peter's, both of which we reproduce (Plates LXV, LXIX). Other pictures show Rome under festive conditions, and we reproduce one delicious vision of the artist himself in his studio in Rome surrounded by vast numbers of his works, and elegantly mixing colours on the minutest of palettes. If he does not give us great art he does at any rate bring out the spirit of Rome in the eighteenth century. He possesses more vitality than Hubert Robert, who belongs to the same school, although the latter is probably superior as an artist.

The modern city has, until the present day, remained in aspect substantially as the Baroque Popes and architects left it. By the beginning of the nineteenth century the wave of fervour was spent, and just as in Venice a lethargy settled down again. Something of essential spiritual quality was gone, and if we look at Turner's paintings and drawings of the city we see how, in spite of his responsiveness to the moods of places, he was puzzled by Rome. In Piranesi's time the great movement was still stirring, and the topographical artist became an integral part of it. Turner, as Dr. Thomas Ashby has demonstrated, was in his most matter of fact temper in his Roman period. The absence of living emotion in the city is a part explanation, but only part, for Venice, in his time a dead city, stirred him profoundly to an inspired drunkenness of colour. It is probable that Turner as a romantic genius never understood the ordered mass of buildings as he understood the disorderly masses of nature : and, as at Venice, effects of light and atmosphere interested him more than the permanency of man-made things under an equable sky. In the oil sketch of the Arch of Constantine in the Tate Gallery he attempts a dazzling Venetian effect, which in view of the subject, is entirely meaningless and inappropriate. In his " View from the Vatican " close by, he attempts to give the real weight and extent of Rome, but fails, becoming merely cumbrous and awkward. The " View from the Vatican " is in a true derogatory sense a *machine*. Most of the water-colours are exact and minute transcripts of the city, but devoid of feeling. Richard Wilson paints Rome with much more appreciation of its static and " eternal " qualities, because he has himself a classical turn of mind, and even Sam Prout in his humble degree was more interested than Turner, finding in Rome the crumbling stones and ruinous dots which his soul loved. Corot, who like Turner specialised also in evasive effects of nature, has like him left an unsatisfactory account of the city. His oil sketches are delightful as oil sketches, but they do not give the essence of Rome.

In fact, the figures of the professional artist and young nobleman sketching under the guidance of his tutor so familiar to us in the engravings of the eighteenth century are replaced in our minds by a new and scientific

26

race.   In the course of the nineteenth century the archæologist came upon the scene, and the great work of excavation began, which has recovered the plan of the Forum and made a scientific reconstruction of the city possible.

With the nineteenth century also came the new orientation of Rome as a civil capital.   The unconscious agency of nationalism, the Napoleonic army entered the city (Plate C), a fact which spurred on the populace, in the manner typical of the Latins in moments of enthusiasm, to proclaim a republic.   The remainder of the tortuous and complicated struggle to establish a nation belongs to the history books.   It may be noticed here that it has had the desired effect of making Rome the vigorous head of a commercial state.   Like the other progressive movements in the history of Rome, the present goes back to the Ancient period.   We have a dictator in the manner of Sulla, an army personally devoted as the ancient armies were, with a pagan dithyramb for a national anthem.   The movement has shoddy features just as in architecture the monument of Victor Emmanuel with its astonishing flamboyance expresses positively the worst of all previous Roman effort.   It is equally unsuitable for transplantation elsewhere.   But it is bound up with the history of the city, and represents a real living force.   All over Rome one hears now the clanking of hammers, and building proceeds with the utmost energy.   And from time to time aeroplanes skim over the Forum and the shadow of a colossal dirigible passes above the Colosseum—a paradoxical reminder of the changing modes of imperial expression.

In his etchings Signor Carbonati gives some of the liveliness of the modern city; and other of our modern artists, like Mr. Cundall, show how the spirit of the twentieth century, by contrast with the nineteenth, finds satisfaction once more in solid and imposing forms.   In fact our illustrations give a whole series of fascinating actions and reactions of city upon artist, and artist upon city, and to bring the lover of topography to this collection with an enhanced interest is the main purpose of this slight study.

PLATE I

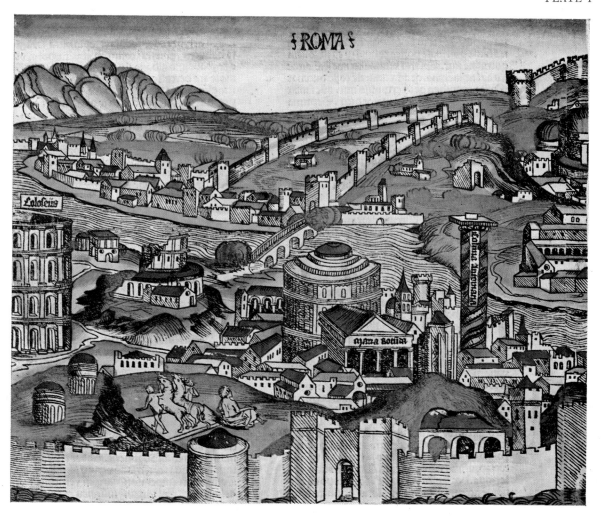

ROMA

VIEW OF ROME. COLOURED WOODCUT
FROM THE NUREMBERG CHRONICLE.

PLATE II

Actual Size

THE VISION AT THE CASTLE OF SAN ANGELO.
FROM THE SFORZA BOOK OF HOURS.

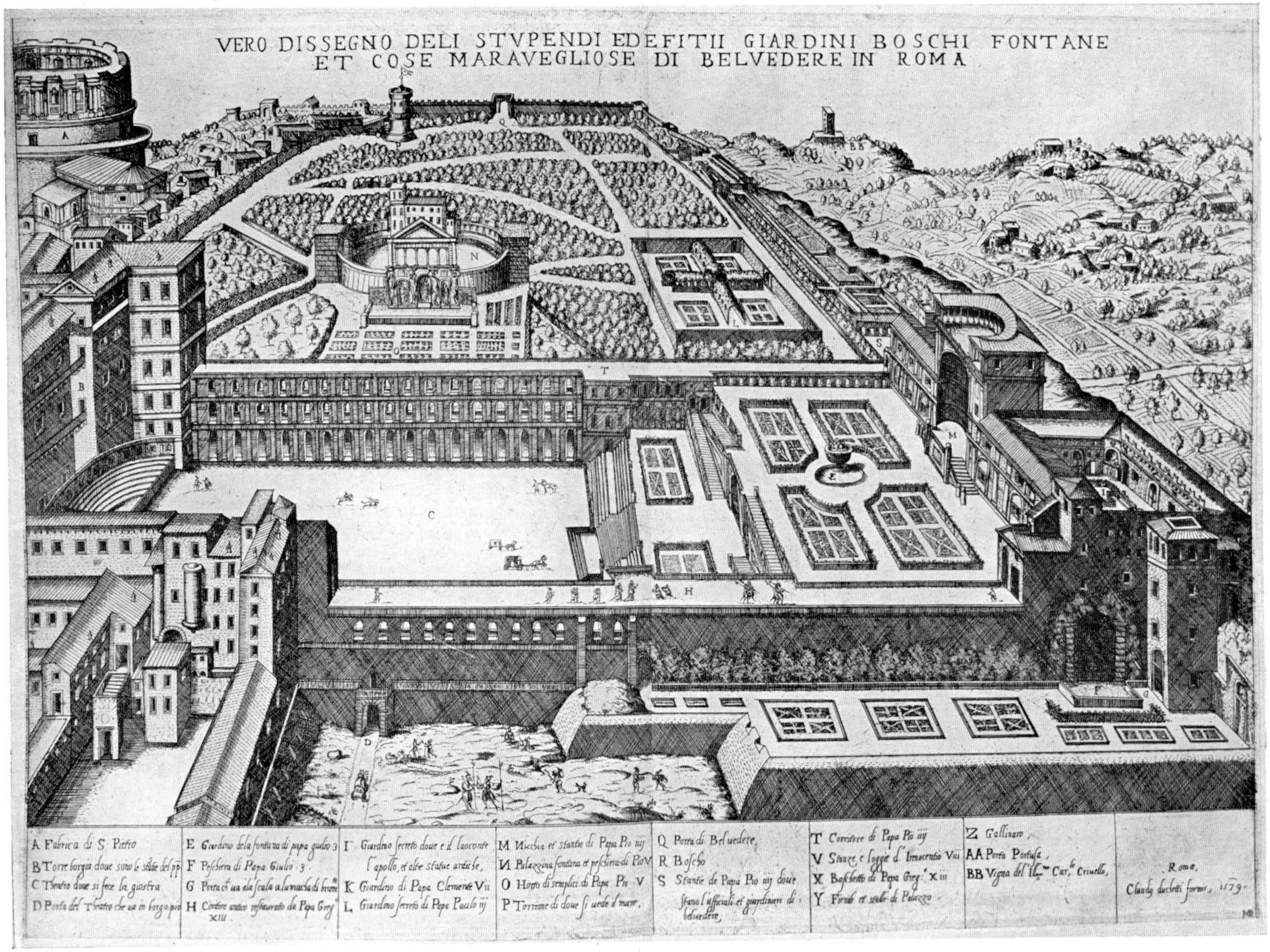

PLATE III

VERO DISSEGNO DELI STVPENDI EDEFITI GIARDINI BOSCHI FONTANE
ET COSE MARAVEGLIOSE DI BELVEDERE IN ROMA

THE GARDENS OF THE BELVEDERE. LINE ENGRAVING BY ANTOINE LAFRERY.

In the Victoria and Albert Museum.

PLATE IV

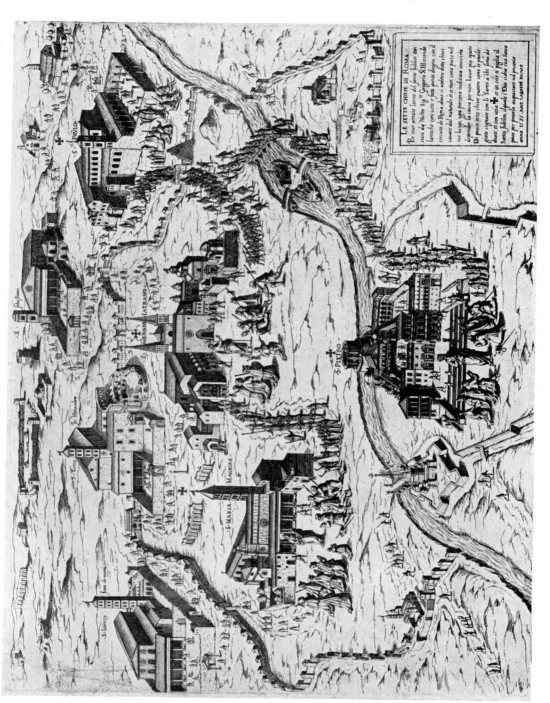

THE SEVEN CHURCHES OF ROME. LINE ENGRAVING BY ANTOINE LAFRERY, 1575.

ABOVE: THE ANTONINE COLUMN.
BELOW: THE TRAJAN COLUMN.
LINE ENGRAVINGS BY ETIENNE DU PERAC.

PLATE VII

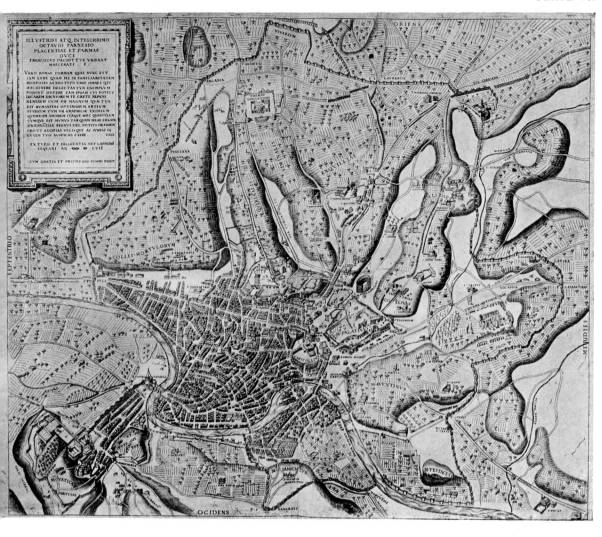

MAP OF THE CITY OF ROME. LINE
ENGRAVING BY ANTOINE LAFRERY.

PLATE VIII

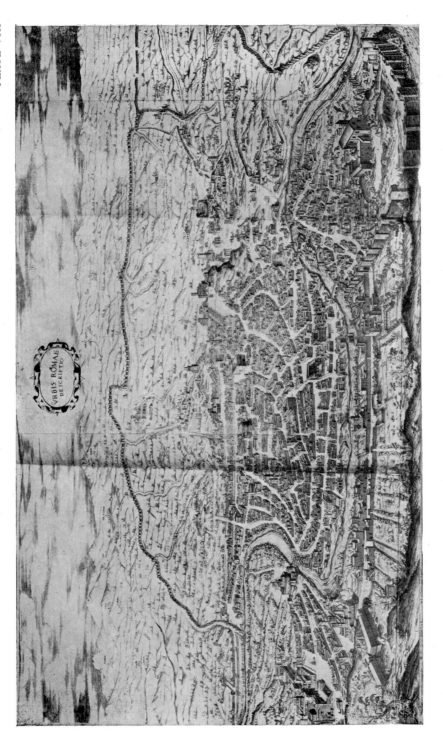

URBIS ROMÆ DESCRIPTIO. LINE ENGRAVING BY ANTOINE LAFRERY.

In the Victoria and Albert Museum.

PLATE IX

MAP OF THE ANCIENT CITY.   LINE ENGRAVING BY ANTOINE LAFRERY.

In the Victoria and Albert Museum.

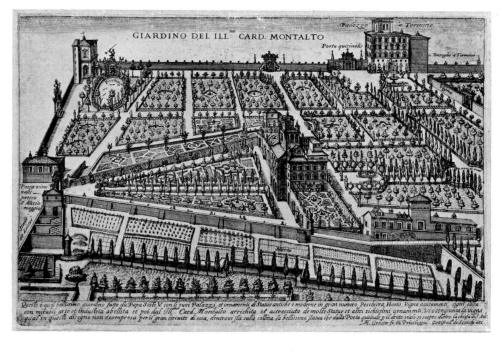

ABOVE: GARDENS OF THE VILLA BORGHESE.
BELOW: GARDENS OF THE VILLA MONTALTO.
LINE ENGRAVINGS BY ETIENNE DU PERAC.

PLATE XII

In the Library of the Royal Institute of British Architects.

THE TEMPLE OF VENUS.   LINE ENGRAVING BY SCAMOZZI.

PLATE XIII

Vestigii del settizimo di Seuero Imperatore, che fu un sepolcro che egli si edificò sopra le strade. Appa, nun per altra caggione, se non che quelli che uenniueno di Africa, lo haueissero negli occhi quello edifitio peitua faccia mea giorno et, tutto di opera Corinthia, con bellissimi colonni, di uarii pietre mischiu parte striatte et parte santye, con li loro membri di martmori, fu chiamato anno settiguso da sette membri dimartmoro, ci che si uede nella parte di dietro Thuulgo lo chiamo Scuola del Virgilio

SEPTIZONIUM.   LINE ENGRAVING BY ETIENNE DU PÉRAC.

In the Victoria and Albert Museum.

PLATE XIV

THE GARDENS OF THE VILLA MEDICI. BY VELASQUEZ.

PLATE XV

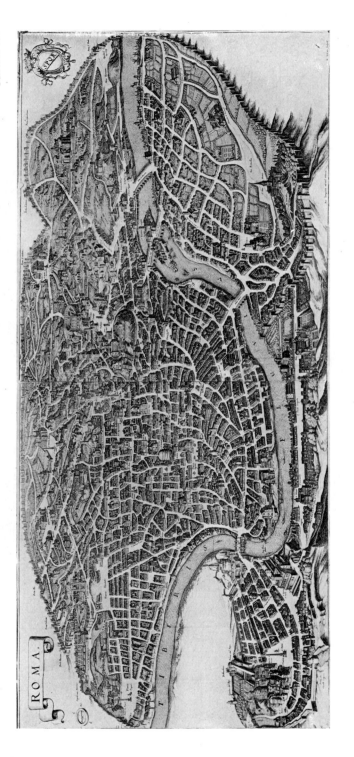

PLAN OF ROME.   LINE ENGRAVING BY M. MORIAN.

In the British Museum.

PLATE XVI

HAEC HABET TEMPLVM IOVIS TONANTIS, TEMPLVM VT QVIDAM PVTANT, CONCORDIAE ARCVM SEPTIMII TEMPLVM IOVIS STATORIS, ET PARTEM COLLIS PALATINI.

THE TEMPLE OF JOVE. LINE ENGRAVING BY SCAMOZZI.

In the Library of the Royal Institute of British Architects.

PLATE XVII

VIEW OF THE FORUM. LINE ENGRAVING BY SCAMOZZI.

In the Library of the Royal Institute of British Architects.

PLATE XVIII

In the Victoria and Albert Museum.　　　APSE OF S.S. GIOVANNI E PAOLO.　DRAWING BY CLAUDE.

PLATE XIX

TOMB OF CÆCILIA METELLA.   DRAWING BY CLAUDE.

PLATE XX

In the British Museum.   RUINED TOWER IN THE CAMPAGNA. DRAWING BY CLAUDE.

PLATE XXI

SENATVS
POPVLVSQVE ROMANVS
DIVO·TITO·DIVI·VESPASIANI·F.
VESPASIANO·AVGVSTO

ARCH OF TITUS. DRAWING BY CLAUDE.

PLATE XXII

THE RIPA GRANDA. DRAWING BY CLAUDE.

PLATE XXIII

THE ARCH OF CONSTANTINE.   DRAWING BY CLAUDE.

PLATE XXIV

PALAZZO ALBANI.   DRAWING BY CLAUDE.

In the Albertina, Vienna.

PLATE XXV

VIE POPULAIRE À ROME.   BY J. BOTH.

In the Rijksmuseum, Amsterdam.

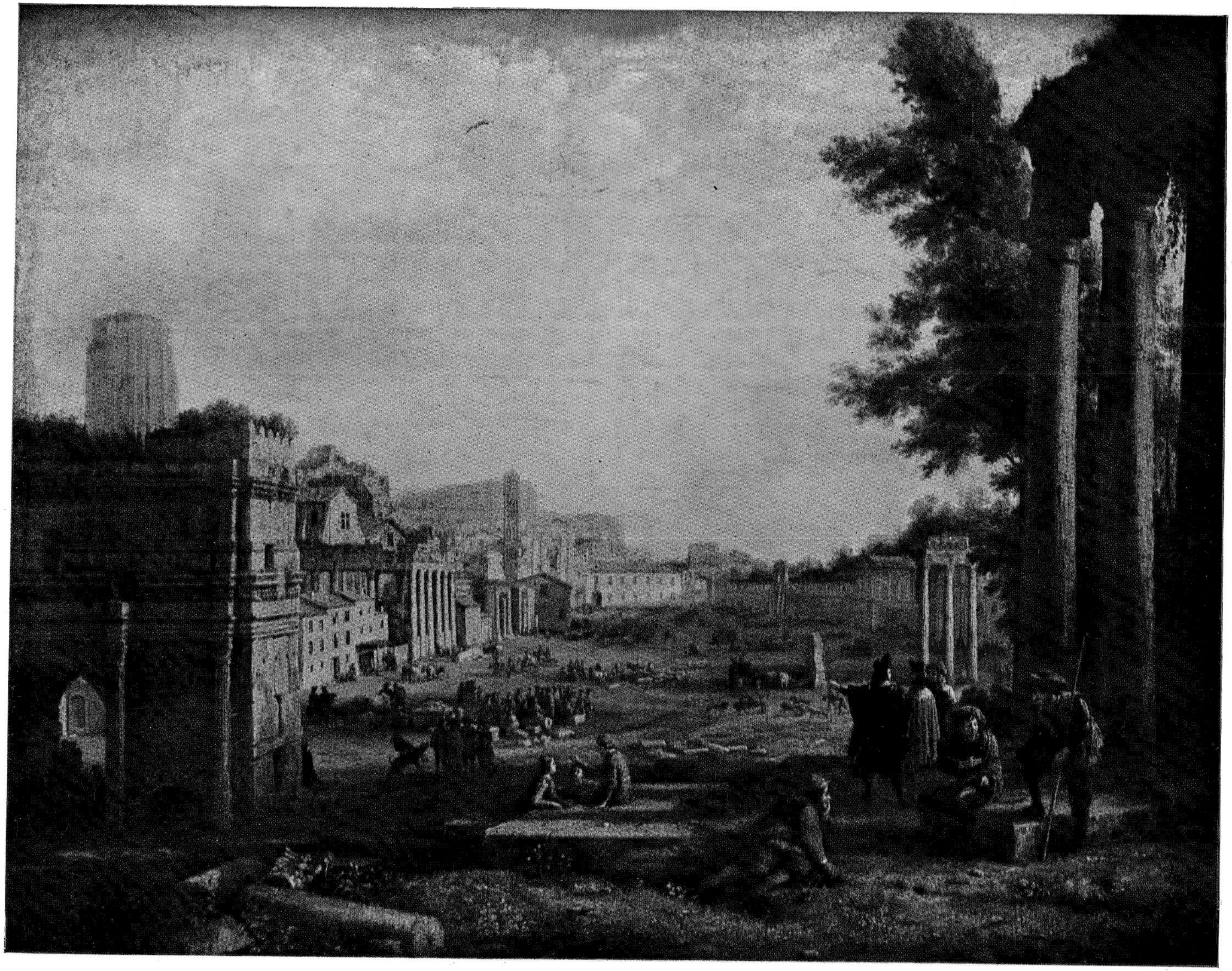

PLATE XXVI

CAMPO VACCINO. BY CLAUDE.

PLATE XXVII

THE ARCH OF DRUSUS. BY JAN AND ANDREAS BOTH.

PLATE XXVIII

SAN GIOVANNI IN LATERANO.   BY G. POUSSIN.

In the collection of the Duke of Devonshire, Chatsworth.

PLATE XXIX

ROME. De borromfie stad van den genfchen aardbodem | ROMA, celeberrima ac fariigeratifima urbs totius orbis.

Pet: Schenk.   Amfield: C.P.

In the possession of A. G. H. Macpherson, Esq.

VIEW OF ROME.   LINE ENGRAVING BY PETER SCHENK.

PLATE XXX

VEDVTA DEL PALAZZO PONTIFICIO AL VATICANO. *Architettura di duecrsi.*

1 Facciata del Palazzo verso le Loggie. 2. Loggie poste nel Cortile. 3. Portico e Colonnato che circonda la Piazza

THE VATICAN. LINE ENGRAVING BY ALESSANDRO SPECCHI.

In the Victoria and Albert Museum.

PLATE XXXI

THE CURIA. LINE ENGRAVING BY ALESSANDRO SPECCHI.

In the Victoria and Albert Museum.

PLATE XXXII

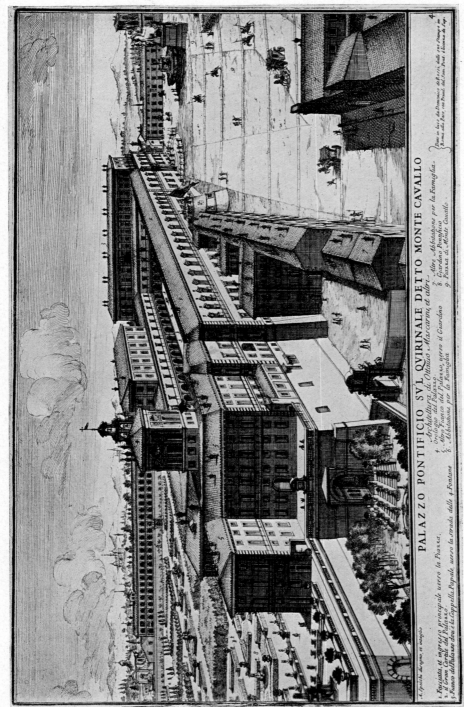

PALAZZO PONTIFICIO SVL QVIRINALE DETTO MONTE CAVALLO

THE QUIRINAL. LINE ENGRAVING BY ALESSANDRO SPECCHI.

In the Victoria and Albert Museum.

PLATE XXXIII

CASTELLO SANTO ANGELO DI ROMA

THE CASTLE OF SAN ANGELO. LINE ENGRAVING BY ALESSANDRO SPECCHI.

PLATE XXXIV

PALAZZO FARNESE DEL SERENIS DVCA DI PARMA.
Architettura di Michelangelo Buonaroti, et Antonio Sangallo, e Giac.º Barozzo da Vignola.
1 Facciata verso la Piazza. 2 Fiamo del medesimo Palazzo verso leuante 3, le due Fontane nella Piazza.
Dato in luce da Domenico de Rossi dalle sue Stampe in Roma alla Pace con Prudegio del Sommo Pontefice e licenza de Superiori

THE FARNESE PALACE. LINE ENGRAVING BY ALESSANDRO SPECCHI.

In the *Victoria and Albert Museum.*

PLATE XXXV

CHIESA DI S·GIROLAMO DELLA NATIONE DE' SCHIAV: NELLA REGIONE DI CAMPO MARZO A RIPETTA

Architettura di Martino Lunghi il uecchio.

1 *Loggia del Palazzo dell'Ecc.:ᵐᵉ Sig:Principe Borghese*   2 *Sbarco de uini et altre merchantie che uengono dalla Sabina.*   38

Gio:Batt:ᵃ Falda dis:et fece   *Pѐ Gio:Iacomo Rossi in roma alla pace cõ priu:del S·Pont:*

SAN GIROLAMO.   LINE ENGRAVING BY ALESSANDRO SPECCHI.

In the Victoria and Albert Museum.

PLATE XXXVI

BASILICA LATERANENSE.   LINE ENGRAVING BY ALESSANDRO SPECCHI.

PLATE XXXVII

PALAZZO DELLA CANCELLERIA FATTO FABRICARE DAL. CARDINAL RAFAELLE RIARIO
Architettura di Bramante da Urbino.
1. Facciata Principale nella Piazza. 2. Fianco del medesimo Palazzo che risponde nella strada del Pellegrino.
dato in luce da Domenico de Rossi dalle sue Stampe in Roma alla Pace con licenza de Sup.

A. Specchi disegno et intaglio.

6

THE CANCELLERIA.   LINE ENGRAVING BY ALESSANDRO SPECCHI.

In the Victoria and Albert Museum.

PLATE XXXVIII

PALAZZO DELL'ECCELLENTIS.ᴬ CASA ALTIERI NELLA PIAZZA DEL GIESV
Architettura di Gio: Antonio de Rossi.
1ᵒVeduta del Palazzo verso il Giesu. 2. Fianco dell'istesso Palazzo verso Ponente.3. Chiesa del Giesu
dato in Luce da Domenico de Rossi dalle sue stampa in Roma alla Pace con Priuil: del S.P. e licenza de Sup

28

THE ALTIERI PALACE.   LINE ENGRAVING BY ALESSANDRO SPECCHI.

In the Victoria and Albert Museum.

PLATE XXXIX

THE GAETANI PALACE. LINE ENGRAVING BY ALESSANDRO SPECCHI.

In the Victoria and Albert Museum.

PLATE XL.

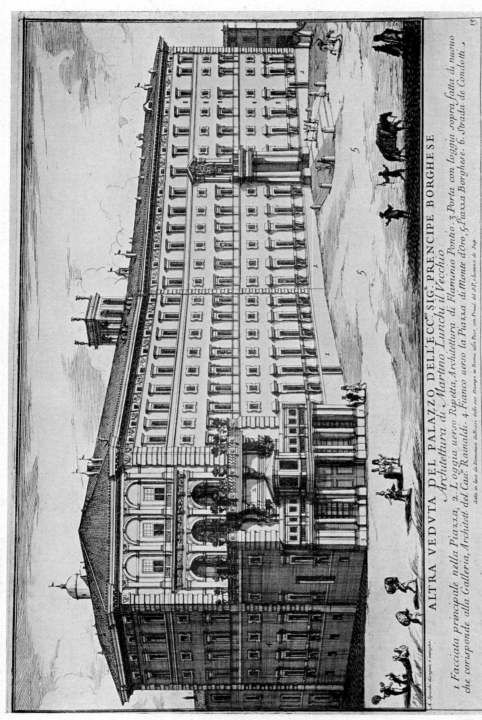

ALTRA VEDVTA DEL PALAZZO DELL'ECC.mo SIG.r PRENCIPE BORGHESE
Architettura di Martino Lunchi il Vecchio

1 Facciata principale nella Piazza, 2. Loggia uerso Ripetta, Architettura di Flaminio Pontio. 3 Porta con loggia sopra fatta di nuouo
che corisponde alla Galleria, Architet: del Caù.r Rainaldi: 4 Fianco uerso la Piazza di Monte d'Oro, 5 Piazxa Borghese. 6. Strada de Condotti.

Data in luce da Domenico deRossI dalle sue Stampe in Roma alla Pace, con Priuil: del S.S. e licenza de Sup

A. Specchi disegnò, e incise.

13

THE BORGHESE PALACE.   LINE ENGRAVING BY ALESSANDRO SPECCHI

In the Victoria and Albert Museum.

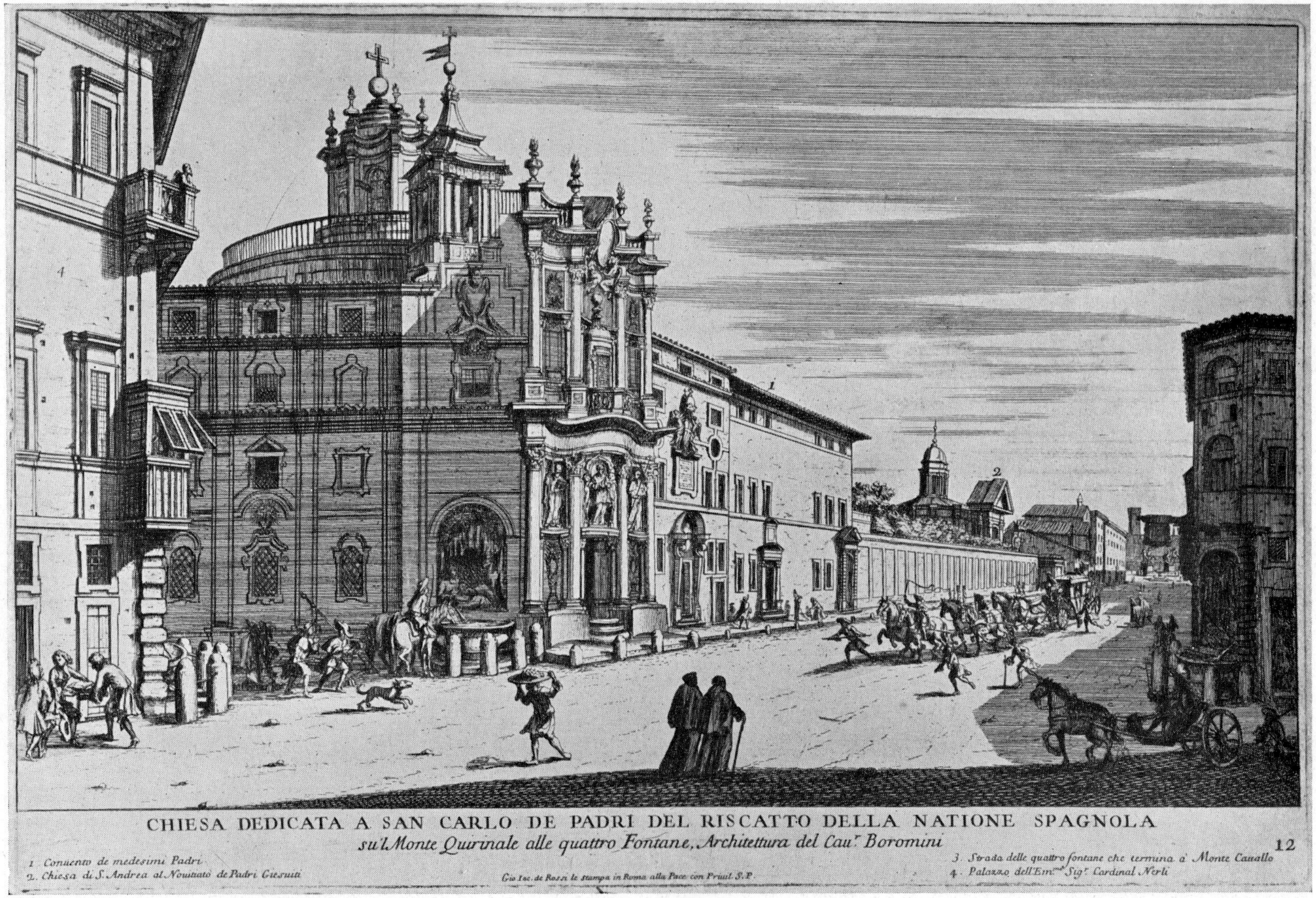

PLATE XLI

CHIESA DEDICATA A SAN CARLO DE PADRI DEL RISCATTO DELLA NATIONE SPAGNOLA
sul Monte Quirinale alle quattro Fontane, Architettura del Cau.r Boromini

CHIESA DI SAN CARLO. LINE ENGRAVING IN ROSSI'S VIEWS OF ROME.

In the Library of the Royal Institute of British Architects.

PLATE XLII

THE CHIGI PALACE.   LINE ENGRAVING BY ALESSANDRO SPECCHI

In the Victoria and Albert Museum.

VEDVTA POSTERIORE DEL MEDEMO PALAZZO BARBERINO CON FACCIATA E SCALA CHE PORTA AL GIARDINO, ET AL PIANO DELLA SALA
Architettura del Caualier Borromino.
1. Giardino con L'Obelisco antco verso le quattro Fontane.

PROSPETTO DEL PALAZZO E PIAZZA DELLA NOBILISIMA FAMIGLIA BARBERINI FATTA da N.S. P. VRBANO VIII
1 Strada che ua alle quattro Fontane 2 Chiesa di S. Nicola di Tolentino 3 Chiesa di S. Maria Maggiore 4 Chiesa di S. Andrea e Coleg: Sorzesei

ABOVE: In the Victoria and Albert Museum. BELOW: In the Library of the Royal Institute of British Architects.

TWO VIEWS OF THE BARBERINI PALACE. LINE ENGRAVINGS FROM ROSSI'S VIEWS OF ROME.

PLATE XLV

VIEW FROM THE CLIVO CAPITOLINO.
ETCHING BY ROSSINI.

PLATE XLVI

THE CASTLE OF SAN ANGELO. LINE ENGRAVING BY FALDA AFTER BERNINI.

PLATE XLVII

FONTANA·NELLA·PIAZZA·DE·SS.ᵗ MATTEI
nel Rione di S.Angelo architettura di Giacomo della Porta.

FONTANA SS. MATTEI.   FROM ROSSI'S VIEWS OF ROME.

In the Library of the Royal Institute of British Architects.

PLATE XLVIII

PIAZZA DEL QUIRINALE. BY KASPAR VANVITELLI.

In the Corsini Palace.

PLATE XLIX

THE VILLA MEDICI. BY KASPAR VANVITELLI.

In the Corsini Palace.

PLATE L

LA TRINITA DEI MONTI. BY KASPAR VANVITELLI.

PLATE LI

CONSPECTVS TEMPLI S.MARIÆ, VVLGO ROTVNDÆ, QVOD OLIM T.IOVIS VLTORIS, SIVE PANTHEON M.AGRIPPÆ.

EXTERIOR OF THE PANTHEON. LINE ENGRAVING BY L. CRUYL.

In the British Museum.

PLATE LII

In the Witt Collection.

THE ARCH OF SEVERUS IN THE LATE XVIth CENTURY.
ANONYMOUS DRAWING OF THE FLEMISH SCHOOL.

PLATE LIII

PIAZZA DEL POPOLO.   LINE ENGRAVING BY G. WOUTERS.

In the British Museum.

PLATE LIV

THE QUIRINAL.   LINE ENGRAVING BY G. WOUTERS.

In the British Museum.

PLATE LV

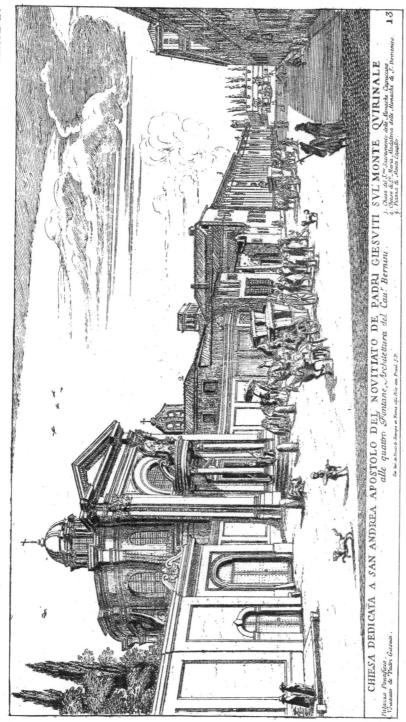

CHIESA DI S. ANDREA APOSTOLO. FROM ROSSI'S VIEWS OF ROME.

In the Victoria and Albert Museum.

PLATE LVI

RAISING THE OBELISK. XVIIth CENTURY LINE ENGRAVING.

PLATE LVII

CHURCH OF S. LORENZO IN MIRANDA. BY CANALETTO.

In the collection of Lord Sandwich.

PLATE LVIII

JUBILEE IN ST. PETER'S, 1700. CONTEMPORARY LINE ENGRAVING.

In the British Museum

PLATE LIX

THE ARCH OF SEVERUS. BY CANALETTO.

PLATE LX

THE PANTHEON.   BY CANALETTO.

PLATE LXI

THE TEMPLE OF CASTOR AND POLLUX.   BY CANALETTO.

ABOVE : PONTE SISTO. BY A.
DEMACHY. *BELOW :* JANICULUM AND
PONTE CESTIO. BY G. VANVITELLI.

PLATE LXIV

CONCERT AT ROME, 1729, ON THE OCCASION OF THE
BIRTH OF A SON TO LOUIS XV.   BY G. PANNINI.

In the Louvre, Paris.

PLATE LXV

THE INTERIOR OF ST. PETER'S. BY G. PANNINI.

In the Louvre, Paris.

(Above): *In the collection of the Duke of Wellington, Apsley House. (Below): In the National Gallery, Dublin.*

ABOVE: THE SPANISH EMBASSY AT ROME. *BELOW:* FÊTE IN THE PIAZZA NAVONA. PAINTINGS BY G. PANNINI.

PLATE LXVIII

THE DUC DE CHOISEUL, FRENCH AMBASSADOR,
LEAVING THE VATICAN.   BY   G.   PANNINI.

In the collection of Lord Ellesmere, Bridgewater House.

PLATE LXIX

THE INTERIOR OF THE PANTHEON. BY G. PANNINI.

PLATE LXX

PIAZZA S. MARIA MAGGIORE. BY G. PANNINI.

PLATE LXXI

Veduta del Tempio di Giove Tonante

TEMPLE OF JUPITER TONANS. ETCHING BY PIRANESI.

In the Library of the Royal Institute of British Architects.

PLATE LXXII

PANNINI'S STUDIO AT ROME.   BY G. PANNINI.

In the collection of : ord Ellesmere, Bridgewater House.

PLATE LXXIII

PIAZZA NAVONA. BY G. PANNINI.

PLATE LXXIV

THE CASTLE OF SAN ANGELO. ETCHING BY PIRANESI.

In the Library of the Royal Institute of British Architects.

PLATE LXXV

PALAZZO ODESCALCHI.   ETCHING BY PIRANESI.

In the Library of the Royal Institute of British Architects.

PLATE LXXVI

Veduta della Facciata della Basilica di S. Croce in Gerusalemme

1. Monastero de Monaci Cistercianci   A Mura moderna fabbricate sulle vestia dell'Anfiteatro Castrense
S. Avanti del Tempio della Speranza Vecchia   Giovani Batista Piranesi Architetto dis: et inc:

In the Library of the Royal Institute of British Architects.

BASILICA DI S. CROCE IN GERUSALEMME.   ETCHING BY PIRANESI.

PLATE LXXVII

THE ARCH OF SEVERUS. ETCHING BY PIRANESI.

In the Library of the Royal Institute of British Architects.

PLATE LXXVIII

PALAZZO DELL'ACCADEMIA.   ETCHING BY PIRANESI.

In the Library of the Royal Institute of British Architects.

PLATE LXXIX

Veduta della Dogana di Terra a Piazza di Pietra

TEMPLE OF NEPTUNE. ETCHING BY PIRANESI.

In the Library of the Royal Institute of British Architects.

PLATE LXXX

THE CASTLE OF SAN ANGELO.   BY C. J. VERNET.

In the National Gallery.

PLATE LXXXI

FONTANA PAOLA. ETCHING BY PIRANESI.

In the Library of the Royal Institute of British Architects.

PLATE LXXXII

THE FORUM OF NERVA.   ETCHING BY PIRANESI.

In the Library of the Royal Institute of British Architects.

PLATE LXXXIII

THE PRONAOS OF THE PANTHEON.   ETCHING BY PIRANESI.

In the Library of the Royal Institute of British Architects.

PLATE LXXXIV

VIEW OF ST. PETER'S. ETCHING BY PIRANESI.

In the British Museum.

PLATE LXXXV

THE COLOSSEUM. ETCHING BY PIRANESI.

In the Library of the Royal Institute of British Architects.

ABOVE: ALBANO NEAR ROME. BELOW: VIEW OF ROME
FROM MONTE MARIO. BY RICHARD WILSON, R.A.

PLATE LXXXVIII

VIEW ON THE TIBER.   DRAWING BY BARTOLOMMEO PINELLI.

ABOVE: PONTE MOLLE. *BELOW:* VILLA
BORGHESE.   DRAWINGS   BY   GOETHE.

PLATE XCI

THE GARDENS OF THE BELVEDERE. BY J. R. COZENS.

PLATE XCII

By courtesy of Mrs. W. Gaunt.

THE THEATRE OF MARCELLUS. ETCHING BY ROSSINI.

PLATE XCIII

THE CHAIR OF ST. PETER. DRAWING BY HUBERT ROBERT.

PLATE XCIV

THE PONTE SAN ANGELO.   DRAWING BY RICHARD WILSON, R.A.

In the possession of A. Kay, Esq.

PLATE XCV

ROME FROM PONTE MOLLE. BY J. P. HACKERT.

By courtesy of Firma Insel-Verlag, Leipzig.

PLATE XCVI

THE TRAJAN FORUM. BY SIR C. L. EASTLAKE, P.R.A.

In the Victoria and Albert Museum.

PLATE XCVII

THE CASCADES OF TIVOLI. BY C. P. FOHR.

In the Frankfort Museum.

PLATE XCVIII

ROME FROM THE VATICAN. PEN AND
WASH DRAWING BY J. M. W. TURNER, R.A.

PLATE XCIX

ST. PETER'S FROM THE SOUTH.
WATER-COLOUR BY J. M. W. TURNER, R.A.

In the National Gallery.

PLATE C

THE FRENCH ARMY ENTERING ROME.
LINE ENGRAVING AFTER NODET.

In the British Museum.

PLATE CI

VIEW OF ROME.   BY DAVID ROBERTS, R.A.

In the National Gallery, Scotland.   (Photo Annan.)

PLATE CII

In the Corsini Palace.

THE CASA MENGARINI.   OIL PAINTING BY IPPOLITO CAFFI.

PLATE CIII

FÊTE IN THE PIAZZA BARBERINI.   BY RICHARD PARKES BONINGTON.

In the May Collection, Paris.

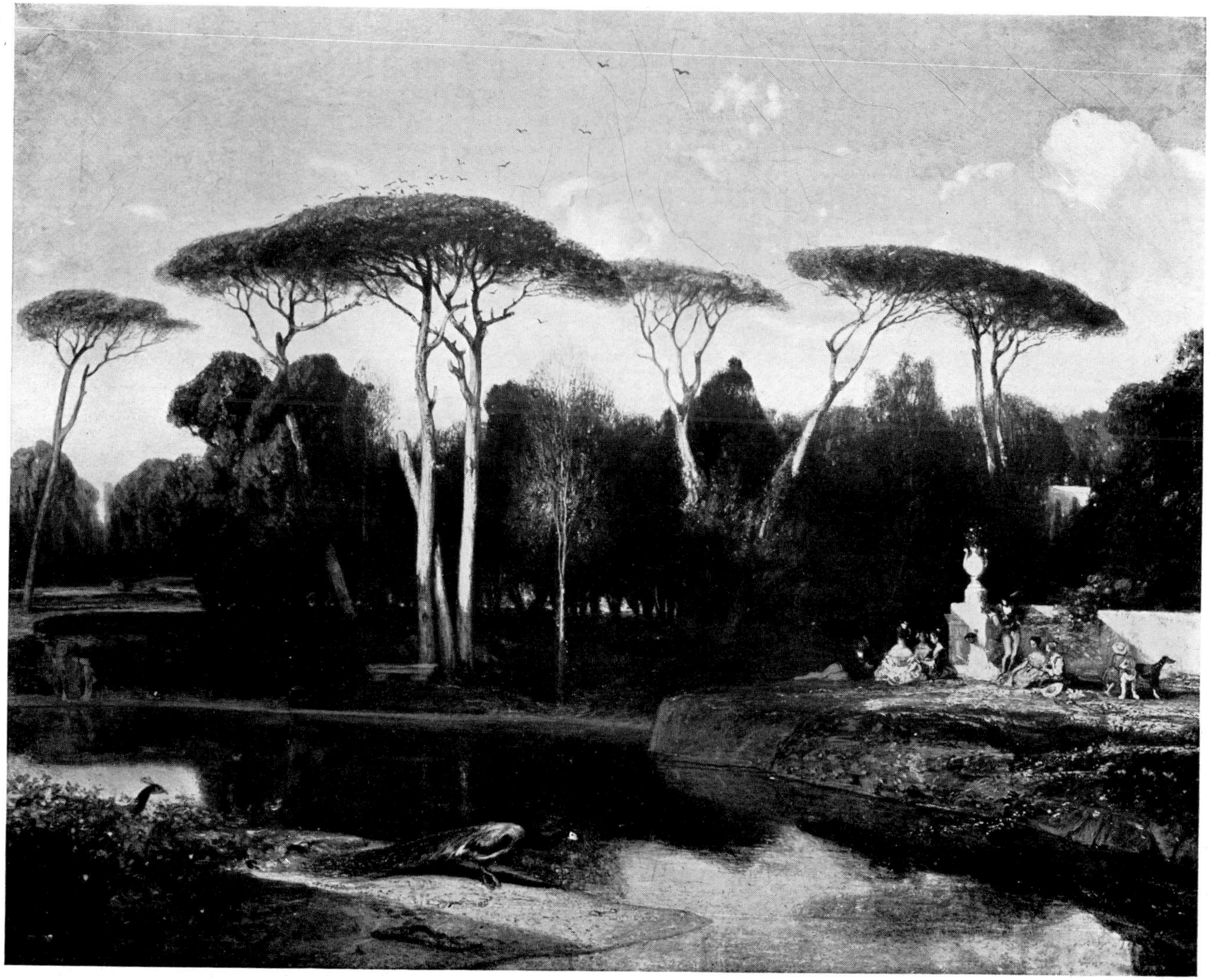

PLATE CIV

GARDEN OF THE VILLA DORIA PAMPHILI. BY A. G. DECAMPS.

PLATE CV

THE FORUM OF NERVA. WATER
COLOUR DRAWING BY S. PROUT.

PLATE CVI

THE PORTICO OF OCTAVIA.
WATER-COLOUR BY S. PROUT.

PLATE CVII

THE TEMPLE OF VESTA. BY FRANZ LENBACH.

In the National Gallery, Berlin.

PLATE CVIII

THE AVENTINE.   DRAWING BY SAMUEL PROUT.

In the possession of Sir Harry Wilson, K.C.M.G., K.B.E.

PLATE CIX

VIEW OF THE COLOSSEUM.   BY J. B. C. COROT.

PLATE CX

THE SPANISH STEPS.   ETCHING BY J. NIXON.

PLATE CXI

THE COLOSSEUM. DRAWING BY J. NIXON.

PLATE CXII

THE FORUM. ETCHING BY LUIGI KASIMIR.

PLATE CXIII

THE ARCH OF TITUS.   COLOURED ETCHING BY LUIGI KASIMIR.

PLATE CXIV

MEDIÆVAL HOUSE. PIAZZA S. CECILIA.
ETCHING BY ANTONIO CARBONATI.

PLATE CXV

10/30

VIA DEL TRITONE.   ETCHING BY ANTONIO CARBONATI.

PLATE CXVI

CAMPANILE DI S. ANDREA.   ETCHING BY ANTONIO CARBONATI

PLATE CXVII

CASA DEI RIENZI. ETCHING BY ANTONIO CARBONATI.

PLATE CXVIII

THE COLONNADE OF ST. PETER'S.
ETCHING BY T. BRENSON.

PLATE CXIX

THE PONTE ROTTO.   ETCHING BY T. BRENSON.

PLATE CXX

THE CAFÉ GRECO.   LITHOGRAPH BY JOHN COPLEY.

From a proof in the possession of Messrs. P. & D. Colnaghi.

PLATE CXXI

THE PALACE OF THE CÆSARS. ETCHING BY T. BRENSON.

PLATE CXXII

In the Victoria and Albert Museum.

PILGRIMS IN THE COLOSSEUM. DRAWING BY VIANELLI.

PLATE CXXIV

WALL OF THE AUGUSTAN FORUM.   BY SYDNEY LEE, A.R.A.

PLATE CXXV

FASCISTI ENTERING ROME.
ETCHING BY HENRY RUSHBURY.

PLATE CXXVI

INTERIOR OF S. MARIA MADDELENA
DRAWING BY WILHELM KIMBEL.

In the collection of Sidney Morse, Esq.

ABOVE: IN THE GARDEN OF THE VILLA PAPA GIULIO.
WATER-COLOUR DRAWING BY W. RUSSELL FLINT,
R.W.S. *BELOW:* GARDENS OF THE VILLA BORGHESE.
WATER-COLOUR DRAWING BY D. S. MACLAUGHLAN.

PLATE CXXIX

PONTE FABRICIO. ETCHING BY R. SCHWABE.

PLATE CXXX

ST. PETER'S.   PENCIL DRAWING BY IAN STRANG.

PLATE CXXXI

THE BASILICA OF CONSTANTINE

THE BASILICA OF CONSTANTINE. ETCHING BY R. SCHWABE

PLATE CXXXII

SS. GIOVANNI E PAOLO.   PEN AND WASH DRAWING BY R. SCHWABE.

PLATE CXXIII

THE FOUNTAIN OF NEPTUNE. BY SIDNEY LEE, A.R.A.

PLATE CXXXIII

THE BATHS OF CARACALLA.   BY SIR D. Y. CAMERON, R.A.

In the possession of Col. D. S. Morton, C.M.G.

PLATE CXXXIV

S. MARIA DELLA PACE.   DRAWING BY ALBERT DECARIS.

PLATE CXXXV

ARCH OF SEVERUS.   LITHOGRAPH BY HOWARD LEIGH.

PLATE CXXXVI

PALAZZO BORGIA. WATER-COLOUR BY CARL LANGHAMMER.

PLATE CXXXVII

THE MAJESTY OF THE CHURCH. ETCHING BY W. WALCOT, R.E.

PLATE CXXXVIII

PORTA DEL POPOLO. WATER-COLOUR BY W. WALCOT, R.E.

By courtesy of Messrs. Ackermann & Son, Ltd.

PLATE CXXXIX

FROM THE PALATINE.   BY C. H. CUNDALL.

PLATE CXL.

CAMPIDOGLIO.   BY   C.   H.   CUNDALL.

PLATE CXLI

THE FORUM.   OIL PAINTING BY C. H. CUNDALL.

PLATE CXLII

By courtesy of D. Croal Thomson, Esq.

PONTE QUATTRO CAPI.   DRAWING BY FRANK BRANGWYN, R.A.

PLATE CXLIII

THE PONTE ROTTO. ETCHING BY FRANK BRANGWYN, R.A.

PLATE CXLIV

PORTA DI S. PAOLO. WOODCUT BY
PROFESSOR GIORGIO PIANIGIANI.